D0756252

WHEN
WALES
WENT TO
WAR
1939–45

Temple Street, Swansea, after a raid in February 1941.

WHEN WALES WENT TO WAR

1939–45

JOHN O'SULLIVAN

SUTTON PUBLISHING

Sutton Publishing Limited
Phoenix Mill · Thrupp · Stroud
Gloucestershire · GL5 2BU

First published 2004

Reprinted 2004, 2005

Copyright © John O'Sullivan, 2004

Unless otherwise stated all photographs in
this book are reproduced courtesy of the
Western Mail and Echo.

**British Library Cataloguing in Publication
Data**
A catalogue record for this book is available from
the British Library.

ISBN 0-7509-3837-4

Typeset in 10.5/13.5pt Plantin.
Typesetting and origination by
Sutton Publishing Limited.
Printed and bound in England by
J.H. Haynes & Co. Ltd, Sparkford.

*This book is dedicated
to world peace*

F.E. Fett of the 77th Heavy Ack-Ack with his wife and daughter. He had just returned from
three years in a Japanese prisoner-of-war camp.

Contents

Dockers unload ammunition from railway trucks at Newport. It was loaded on to the SS *Stanrealm* but the vessel's destination was a secret.

Sounds of War

by PAUL FLYNN MP

Paul Flynn, Labour MP for Newport West since 1987, was only five in January 1941 when the Germans brought death and destruction to Grangetown, Cardiff, where he was living with his parents James and Kathleen, his brothers Terry and Michael and his three-day-old sister Mary.

My father's brother Ted was a special constable charged with guarding Canton Bridge over the River Taff during air raids. Dutifully he hurried from his Pentre Gardens home to the bridge between Cardiff Castle and Sophia Gardens at the bidding of the siren on the evening of 2 January 1941. No one ever told him how to guard the bridge. If the Germans parachuted out of the sky, he had no weapon to defend it. Ruefully he concluded that his job was to spot bombs that were about to hit the bridge, catch them and throw them in the River Taff.

Our infant inability to feel the depths of grief shielded us from the worst suffering of war. We accepted the empty desks at St Patrick's school the morning after a bomb destroyed four houses in Paget Street killing two classmates. Worse horrors were ahead. Landmines wiped out entire neighbourhoods in Grangetown and Riverside.

There was the rich excitement of watching a dogfight as planes fought at midday. It was the day after a flight by a German spotter plane to photograph the destruction of the night's raid. Roaring engines, the crackle of guns and cotton wool puffs of smoke formed a wonderful drama above our heads.

We experienced the raids through the sounds of guns and bombs and the vibration of explosions. When a bomb was heard, beginning with its screaming fall to earth, there was a ritual bowing of heads. Bodies braced themselves for a possible impact. The scream grew louder, sharper. Boom! Relief and mutual congratulations that we were in the right place, again. Alive. Untouched. Wise heads would then

Paul Flynn MP.

announce, 'That one was close' as they guessed the distance from the sound and flash.

The master plan was that families should remain in their shelters all night. Cold and discomfort drove us back to our beds as soon as the all-clear siren sounded. For ease of possible escape we slept downstairs. Following our return to our beds after one raid, we were woken by my mother because there was a strong smell of gas. She opened the windows to let it out. That did not help. A time-bomb had severed the gas main in the road six houses distant from ours. A passing lorry set off the bomb. There was an almighty explosion. A sheet of flame 50 feet high roared above our three-storey homes. Even at 30 yards distance the heat was unbearable. Only my baby sister Mary, who was born just three days earlier, slept through the ordeal. We children were moved out of the bombed area into Granny Edwards' house in Caerphilly, where we continued to pull her leg about the man's cloth cap – known to us as a dai cap – that she was wearing. It is a memory as vivid as the sounds of war that rocked our childhood.

Paul Flynn MP
Newport, 2004

Let's Not Forget

Welsh troops have been in the front line in conflicts throughout history and the Second World War was no exception. From the time that Hugh Rowlands from Gwynedd won the first Victoria Cross by throwing a live shell from the deck of his ship in the Crimea War to the Second World War when Welshmen were winning honours at sea, in the air and on the battlefields of Europe and Asia, Wales has produced many heroes. But it is not just the deeds of the men who won Victoria and George Crosses that deserve to be remembered. Men and women of all ranks, civilian and military, played key roles in battles at home and overseas. It has been my privilege to know some of them personally, including Billy James, Billy Baker and Wilf Wooller, all members of the Cardiff-based Sportmen's Battalion, the 77th Heavy Ack-Ack, who spent three years in Japanese prisoner-of-war camps. Their story is the kind of which legends are made.

I also knew – and played bowls with – a Barry man who had a £10,000 price put on his head after leading a guerrilla army in Burma. Thousands of families have personal memories of the war and the part played by their relatives. I have the opportunity in these pages to write about my father's humble role. The son of Tim O'Brien, whose story is told on p. 4, was in the same class, football and cricket teams and choir as me at St Helen's School and church, Barry. George Morgan, who survived shark-infested seas after the sinking of the heavy cruiser HMS *Cornwall* in 1942, was married to my elder sister Pat and at a surprise party for his eightieth birthday at the Glenbrook Hotel, Barry, I presented him with a *This is Your Life* account of the sea battle, including copies of photographs taken from Japanese aircraft as the two cruisers sank. As a schoolboy during the war I belonged to an accordion band and concert party which entertained troops and civilians. I also have vivid memories of air raids, American troops leaving the town to take part in the D-Day landings and the street parties at the end of the war. For me this book is both a personal and professional journey.

Part One tells a story that some authorities didn't want told. It's the story of the German air raids that brought death and destruction to Cardiff and other parts of Wales during the Second World War. The story of the part played by German spies and members of Hitler's Nazi Party who had connections with Wales and whose evil deeds helped to plan the raids. The story of the notorious Nazi who lived in Cardiff in the 1930s and was hanged for treason. The reason why Cardiff was chosen as the target to revenge the Dam Busters raid on Germany.

The City Council wanted to ban the story being told at an event to mark the sixtieth anniversary of the last air raid on Cardiff, for fear that it might upset the German consul based in the city. She made it clear in an interview with the *South Wales Echo* that she had no objections. When I revealed to the *Echo* in May 2003 the City Council's decision to ban the story of the blitz there was an incredible reaction from readers. There were pages of letters of support for my proposal that the whole truth should be told. The demand came not only from the older generation who had their memories of the war but also from schoolchildren wanting to know what had happened to their city. The council changed its mind and the presentation went ahead in front of more than 200 people at the City Hall on 21 May 2003. After a moving memorial service conducted by the lord mayor's chaplain, the Revd Stewart Lisk, my former BBC colleague Vincent Kane and myself acted as narrators for the story, which is expanded here to tell of the raids throughout Wales, especially at Swansea, Newport and Pembroke Dock. Some of what appears in the pages that follow was included in a *Western Mail and Echo* booklet called *Bombers Over Wales*, published in the late 1940s. The rest has come from my research during the fifty years I have worked as a journalist in South Wales.

The second part of this book brings together stories relating to the people of Wales and the war, at home and overseas, including the Welsh sportsmen who were forced to build the notorious Burma railway while prisoners of the Japanese, the heroic deeds of the Victoria Cross winners connected with Wales, the bravery of the ARP wardens and others who stepped into the breach at home, and the moving story of a Merchant Navy captain from Wales who was found alive on a remote island after being reported killed in action.

One of the greatest men I knew during my fifty years as a journalist was Group Captain Leonard Cheshire VC, who opened one of his care homes in Cardiff in the 1960s. Cheshire was the official British observer when the Americans dropped an atomic bomb on the Japanese city of Nagasaki. I visited Nagasaki in 1973 and one of the people I met was a woman who had lost all her family in the atomic bomb raid. I asked who she blamed. She struck her chest and said: 'Mea culpa, mea culpa.' ('My fault, my fault.') I asked her what she meant. Through an interpreter she told me that she had not prayed hard enough for peace. She spent eight hours a day praying in church.

I hope that those reading this book, which has been written not to glorify war but to remind people of the sacrifices made, will join me and also pray for peace.

John O'Sullivan
Cardiff
6 June 2004, the sixtieth anniversary of D-Day

PART ONE

The Blitz

Above: Constellation Street, Riverside, where five houses were destroyed and three people killed in the raid in October 1940. *Below:* Grangetown residents salvaging possessions from bombed homes after a raid, January 1941.

Introduction

A total of 984 people were killed and 1,221 seriously injured during the air raids on Wales during the Second World War. In Cardiff there were 575 red alerts, which meant there were enemy raiders overhead. Swansea, which suffered more than any other part of the principality, had 578 red warnings.

Between June 1940 and May 1943, 2,155 high-explosive bombs were dropped on the coastal and valley towns of South Wales. Of these 299 failed to explode. Some 37 parachute mines were dropped and 53 special bombs, including phosphorous and oil missiles, found targets. It is estimated that up to 50,000 incendiaries rained from the skies.

The Barry, Wenvoe and Rhoose districts were bombed on twenty-three occasions. Penarth, Dinas Powis, Llandough, Leckwith and Sully had fourteen attacks, the most serious being on 4 March 1941, when 100 high explosives crashed on Penarth, killing five people and seriously injuring twenty-nine.

RAF St Athan was bombed eighteen times and Llantwit Major twenty-three times. Nearly 100 high explosives and more than 6,000 incendiaries were dropped on Whitchurch, Rhiwbina and Lisvane in a total of eighteen raids. The key target was the Royal Ordnance Factory at Llanishen, which suffered little damage until it was hit by a British shell, which killed nine workers.

The Rhondda had six raids. The most tragic was on 29 April 1941 when twenty people were killed at Cwmparc as high explosives and two parachute mines fell on miners' cottages. Four young evacuees were among those who died. Nurse Elizabeth Jones of Treorchy was the only Glamorgan Civil Defence person to die in the air raids. She was caring for injured in a house in Cwmparc which received a direct hit, killing all the occupants.

TOTAL CASUALTIES IN ALL AIR RAIDS ON WALES

	killed	seriously injured		killed	seriously injured
Swansea	387	412	Denbighshire	18	10
Cardiff	355	502	Carmarthenshire	14	13
Newport	51	63	Caernarvonshire	5	14
Glamorgan	82	120	Flintshire	2	6
Pembrokeshire	45	42	Anglesey	0	3
Monmouthshire	25	36	**Total**	**984**	**1,221**

Cardiff under Attack

After the collapse of France the people of Cardiff, like every other seaside community, lived on the edge of a volcano. Air raids were expected daily. It was just before midnight on 19 June 1940 that enemy aircraft alert sirens first sounded over the city. It was a spying mission by the German Luftwaffe.

Cardiff suffered its first fatal casualties on 9 July 1940, when a lone bomber swooped over the docks and landed a direct hit on a ship carrying timber. The bomb exploded in one of the holds of the *San Felipe* and seven men were killed.

Tim O'Brien (in the hat) and his son Richard who is standing in front of him. *(Jean O'Brien)*

After the tragedy Tim O'Brien, a burly docker of David Street, was hailed a hero. On that sunny afternoon Tim the Devil didn't hesitate and went into the bomb-damaged smoke-filled hold. One fatally injured man, who was blinded in the attack, shouted for help. Tim, a gentle giant, lifted him into a tub that other dockers had lowered into the belly of the ship. Tim held the man in his arms while the two of them were hauled out but the crewman died later.

Twice more Tim went into the hold and brought injured men to the deck. Tim, who had carried a wounded solider 600 yards to safety in the First World War, was awarded an industrial medal for his bravery at Cardiff Docks. Later he was steward of the Glamorgan Wanderers Club before he became landlord of the Royal Hotel at Cadoxton, Barry.

One man was killed in Portmanmoor Road, Splott, on 24 August 1940. Two days later houses in Crichton Street, North Street and Homfray Street, were damaged by bombs. One woman was killed and nineteen people were injured.

On 22 August, five Cardiff firemen died while helping to tackle burning oil tanks at Pembroke Dock, which were bombed on the 19th. The fire was the biggest of the war in Wales and the Germans returned on a second day to machine-gun some of the firefighters, but not the brave men from Cardiff. The story of their deaths was related by Home Office official Tom Breaks. He told an inquest how the men were 20 feet in front of him at work with a fire jet. 'Suddenly, there was a large burst of flame which seemed to envelop them,' he said. 'The last I saw of them was when they were retreating from the huge tongues of flame which shot out from everywhere.' The Cardiff firemen who died were Clifford Mills (30) of Brunswick

Two views of the bomb-damaged timber vessel *San Felipe* following the first fatal raid on Cardiff, 9 July 1940.

Street, Frederick Davies (31) of Llanbradach Street, Ivor Kilby (29) of Gelligaer Street, Trevor Morgan (31) of May Street and John Thomas of Elaine Street. The city and Wales mourned them.

Many people who lived in the area of Albany Road were the victims of a vicious raid on 3 September 1940 – exactly one year to the day after Britain declared war on Germany. One house in Arabella Street was cut from adjoining premises as if by a gigantic knife. A family by the name of Waters was buried under the debris and rescue parties struggled in the darkness to reach the victims. Angus Street, Moy Road and Woodville Road were also targeted while an oil-bomb set three houses in Claude Road on fire. Eleven people, including six children, were killed and thirty-five were injured in that raid.

That same week in September 1940 the Cardiff ice-house (the building at the docks used for storing imported meat and fruit, and also known as the Welsh Cold

Albany Road, where two people died during a raid on 3 September 1940.

Cardiff ice-house, where fruit and meat were stored, was gutted by fire during a raid in September 1940.

Store) was gutted and the Tresilian Hotel was damaged in an air raid. Two bombs also landed in Westgate Street between the flats and the Angel Hotel. On 15 September five people died when bombs fell on Orbit Street and Wordsworth Avenue. Five houses in Constellation Street were destroyed during a raid on 10 October.

In total some 864 high-explosive bombs and 2,410 incendiaries fell on South Wales in the autumn and winter of 1940, but this was only a grim rehearsal for the blitz, which came with a vengeance to Cardiff on a cold starry night in 1941.

THE WORST RAID

There was a full moon on the freezing evening of 2 January 1941. The siren sounded at exactly 6.37 p.m. and within minutes hundreds of incendiary bombs were falling in all parts of the city. The fire-bombs performed their dance of death in Leckwith Wood, the castle grounds and Sophia Gardens. The open spaces saved

Above: A butcher's shop at the corner of Trinity Street. *Below:* A bomb disposal squad in Cardiff.

the city from further destruction, for seventy small explosive bombs fell on Leckwith Wood and Common, where earlier incendiaries had marked a false target for the Luftwaffe. Observers believed that the navigators had been confused by the two rivers, the Ely and the Taff.

Other incendiaries placed the city in a spotlight and the Portland stone buildings in the civic centre looked like a giant wedding cake. A few bombs were smothered on the roof of the City Hall but little damage was done to the main buildings in the centre. Brave men and boys kicked fire-bombs into the Glamorganshire Canal, but the fire-storm created by the first wave of bombers caused serious damage in other parts of the city. The firefighters dealt with 170 calls that night. Major buildings destroyed or severely damaged included Bristow Wadley's premises in Mill Lane; Noah Rees Warehouse in Working Street, Canton Secondary School, Leyland Rubber Works in Harrowby Lane and the Paint Works at East Canal Wharf. Firemen bravely fought the outbreaks but faced a growing problem. Between 7 p.m. and 7.30 p.m. buildings in St John Square went up in flames. Peacocks Bazaar in Queen Street was burnt out and the Corporation Transport Offices in Paradise Place were destroyed. There were also extensive fires at the Cavendish Furniture Warehouse in Tudor Road and the timber yard in North Morgan Street. In spite of the problems, every blaze was subdued by midnight, thanks to the dedication of the fire service.

It was shortly after 7 p.m. that the first high-explosive bomb fell in Grangetown, resulting in one of the most tragic incidents of the war. A number of people – the

The site of the Conservative Club in Neville Street, Grangetown.

exact figure is not known – were killed in a private shelter which received a direct hit. This shelter was the basement of Hollyman's Bakery on the corner of Corporation Road and Stockland Street, where Clarence hardware store stands. The bodies were not recovered and a plaque marking the last resting place of the victims was placed on the site in 2001.

The Grangetown Gas Works were hit too, adding to problems caused throughout the city by broken gas mains. The main water pipes were also damaged, which explains why water supplies were rationed, with householders collecting supplies from standpipes and tankers in various areas. Nuns from Nazareth House drew their supplies from tankers in Maindy Stadium. Electricity supplies were also affected and the Cardiff Royal Infirmary and the City Lodge – later known as St David's Hospital – were among the buildings without power. High explosives fell in Wembley Road, Ninian Park Road, Neville Street, De Burg Street and Blackstone Road. Scores of people were killed or injured.

Llandaff Cathedral, Cardiff, was hit by a parachute mine in January 1941.

The scene that greeted worshippers at Llandaff Cathedral after the raid. The rebuilding work was not completed until many years after the war ended.

Seven people died in one house in Neville Street and a whole funeral party was wiped out during a wake at a house in Blackstone Road. Many streets in Riverside were flattened, with huge craters marking the sites of demolished houses. Part of a motor car was found hanging from a lamppost in Neville Street. Civil Defence workers risked their lives to help the stricken people, and women ambulance drivers ignored the bombs to ferry injured men, women and children to hospital. The Riverside Conservative Club was destroyed but a photograph of Winston Churchill found in the rubble was presented to the Prime Minister when he visited Cardiff in April 1941.

Shortly before 8 p.m. All Saints' Church in Llandaff North was destroyed by fire and it was generally believed that this provided a beacon for the Luftwaffe to target Llandaff Cathedral, which was badly damaged by a parachute mine. St Michael's College, Llandaff, was also hit as were houses in Prospect Drive, Ely Road and Fairwater Road.

The Germans scored a direct hit on the famous Cardiff Arms Park in January 1941.

Unexploded parachute mines were reported in the castle grounds, Crawshay Lane, Ninian Park Road, the railway embankment near De Croche Place and on an allotment off Caerphilly Road, where a group of six civilians tried to pull the monster from the crater it had made. They wrongly thought it was part of a German bomber that had been shot down. Royal Navy and Royal Engineers bomb disposal experts made the unexploded mines safe. They had to blow up some of them where they fell, causing unavoidable damage to nearby houses.

A parachute mine that did explode fell on the famous Arms Park rugby ground, causing considerable damage to the stands and terraces. It landed near the Riverside goalposts and caused a crater 14 feet deep and 50 feet in diameter. The Lyne Grandstand, built at a cost of £20,000 and formally opened when Wales played England in 1934, was virtually destroyed. The roof was blasted away and the seating badly damaged. The large concrete enclosure at the Riverside end was also wrecked.

A few small bombs and scores of incendiaries hit Ninian Park football ground. Among the troops who tackled them were the Cardiff Sportsmen's Battalion, the

77th Heavy Ack-Ack Regiment Royal Artillery, which had a base at Sloper Road Park. The battalion included some of the best-known players from the fields of rugby, soccer, cricket and other sports. They included cricket ace and rugby player Wilf Wooller and Cardiff City's Billy James, Billy Baker, Ernie Curtis and Bobby Tobin. In the early years of the war the men kept morale high by playing matches to entertain the people of South Wales, but in 1942 the battalion was sent to Java, was captured *en bloc* by the Japanese and spent the next three years in Japanese prisoner-of-war camps. Their story is told in the second part of this book (see p. 70).

The 1941 raid started at 6.37 p.m. on 2 January and the all-clear did not sound until 4.50 a.m. on the 3rd. The city was under constant attack for more than 10 hours. Sources say that Cardiff was struck by 111 German bombers that night; they dropped 115 tons of high explosive. A total of 165 people were killed in the raid and 168 suffered serious injuries. Another 240 needed treatment for minor injuries. Some 95 houses were totally destroyed and 233 were so badly damaged that they had to be demolished. A further 426 homes were declared uninhabitable until repairs could be carried out. Thousands of others had windows blown out or roofs or chimneys damaged. Hundreds of families had to be evacuated from their homes and looked after in schools and churches, which were turned into rest

The Cardiff Home Guard Band on parade outside the City Hall during the war.

centres. Emergency services dealt with fires, unexploded bombs and unsafe buildings. As dawn broke it was so cold that the water froze in the fire hoses. But the citizens of Cardiff lived up to the spirit of a message sent by King George VI in a radio broadcast to the nation in the spring of 1941. He said: ''Tis not the walls that make the city, but the people who live within them.'

One episode from that night could have been a scene from the TV programme *Dad's Army*. Cardiff's Home Guard was gathered at the Continental Restaurant in Queen Street waiting for the top brass to arrive when the siren sounded. All thoughts of a pleasant night out disappeared. Edwin Price, who lived in Boverton Street, told me in a letter in 1978 that he and other members of the Home Guard were sent to various parts of the city as the Germans launched their attack on Cardiff. Edwin and his team were dispatched to the old Cardiff High School for Girls in The Parade where there was an ARP post. They were blown down the steps into the basement as a landmine* fell in nearby Talworth Street.

At Talworth Street, Edwin found a fire engine from Bargoed in the Rhymney Valley. Its equipment did not fit the Cardiff hydrants. The Home Guard went into a house where a blaze had started because the blast had scattered the coal fire over the living room. A bucket chain was set up to tackle the outbreak but they had difficulty lifting the bucket over the kitchen sink, so one bright spark unscrewed the tap to allow the water to flood the area and douse the flames. After the fire was under control they couldn't find the tap – so they whittled down a stick to plug the hole in the wall. In the light of the next day they found that the sink was in one house and the fire in the neighbouring building. The Home Guard had gained entry by a hole in the wall caused by the blast.

Edwin recalled another incident when the commanding officer of his group got tough with men who wore Home Guard issue boots to work. He carpeted one suspect (it could have been Pike of *Dad's Army*) and read the riot act to him. He then demanded to know what work the boy did for a living that warranted the sturdy footwear. 'I'm a hairdresser – in a ladies' salon,' answered the lad.

It was not only the Cardiff Home Guard who had problems with boots. In April 1941 the Ministry of Supply reported that it was unable to meet the requirements of many of the South Wales miners who served in the Home Guard. The reason for this was that scores of miners took size 5 footwear and there were no boots that small available. The men were told to use the boots they wore underground.

Hundreds of children were evacuated from Cardiff following the blitz of January 1941. Within 24 hours of the bombs raining down on Grangetown, Bill Bowen's

---

* Some confusion seems to have arisen in the use of the terms landmine and parachute mine. Were they the same weapon or were they different? Martin Garnet, a weapons expert at the Imperial War Museum in London, said 'landmines' were in fact German naval mines which were adapted to be dropped on targets with the aid of parachutes. The first deliberate use in Britain of the naval parachute mine, the *Luftmine*, was on 16 September 1940. They soon came to be called landmines by the British. The landmines used in many corners of the world in the late twentieth and early twenty-first centuries were generally magnetic booby traps planted by mine-laying machines.

mother had packed her bags and taken her four children to the safety of the mining village of Aberfan, 24 miles away. The village made world headlines on 21 October 1966, when 116 children and 28 adults were killed as an avalanche of coal slurry destroyed a school and many houses, but in 1941 it was a safe haven for children escaping the Cardiff blitz.

The Bowen family had been living in Clyde Street, Cardiff, within yards of where people had been killed and injured in the worst blitz to hit the city during the war. Bill's father had died in 1935 and his mother, Olive Warren, had remarried. Her second husband was in the army, serving in the Faroe Islands. Mrs Bowen had relatives in the Aberfan area, and she and her three sons and daughter crowded into a small terraced house for a few nights before being offered homes by other families.

Bill, who was to become chairman of South Glamorgan County Council in 1991, was only ten at the time of the blitz. He went to Pant Glas School, Aberfan, which was destroyed in the 1966 landslide. 'We lived in Aberfan for

Bill Bowen.

two years, and I was confirmed by Archbishop Michael McGrath in St Benedict's Church,' said Bill, who in the 1990s was knighted by the Pope for his service to local government and Catholic education. 'Aberfan was a culture shock for us. The village was surrounded by coalmines in those days and life was so different to what we had known in Cardiff. But the people opened their homes and hearts to us and we were safe from the bombing.' But the Germans came close on one occasion when they bombed a house in the neighbouring village of Mount Pleasant, killing four members of one family – the only deaths from bombing in the Merthyr borough during the war. Bill Bowen and his family returned to Cardiff in the early part of 1943, only weeks before the Germans launched their last raid against the city on 18 May.

Grangetown people were used to wartime tragedies: 21-year-old Stoker First Class William Welton, an old boy of St Patrick's School, was the first Cardiff citizen to be killed in action in the First World War. He was serving on HMS *Amphion*, which sunk with the loss of all hands after hitting a mine in the North Sea on 6 August 1914, when the war was only two days old.

When the lord mayor of Cardiff, Alderman Charles McCale, asked an elderly widow in Grangetown how she was coping with the air raids in 1941 she told him: 'Well it's like this. I have a tot of whisky and then read my favourite passage in the

Bible. This comforts me, so I tuck my head under the pillow and say to myself, now to hell with Hitler!' In April 1942 a Grangetown man was fined £3 – probably more than a week's wages - for walking out of a lecture on how to deal with fire-bombs.

The lord mayor spoke movingly at the January council meeting that followed the 1941 raid in which 165 men, women and children had been killed. He gave heartfelt sympathy to the grieving families and prayed for the recovery of the scores of injured people.

The chief constable of Cardiff praised the exemplary courage and efficiency of the police, fire service – including crews from many corners of South Wales – wardens, Civil Defence workers, ambulance drivers, doctors, nurses, Home Guard and voluntary workers. He saved his finest thoughts for the 'cool and fearless' conduct of the general public. The council also passed a vote of sympathy at the recent death of a freeman of Cardiff, the founder of the Boy Scouts, Lord Baden Powell.

No Let-up

In the early months of 1941 South Wales was under constant attack from the German air force. The centre of Swansea was virtually destroyed and Newport also suffered severe damage. In Cardiff on 13 January one man was killed at Cowbridge Road and a second at Llanbleddian Gardens. On 19 January a woman was killed in Oakfield Street. On 2 February three members of the same family were killed in Senghennydd Road and only outstanding action by a fire-watcher saved the City Hall from severe damage. Ronald Brignall of Cartwright Lane, Fairwater, was commended by the City Council for dealing with an incendiary bomb that landed on the roof of the City Hall. There was also praise for the soldiers who left their base in the Embassy Hall in Cathays to help in the rescue work that night.

On Ash Wednesday, 27 February, 19-year-old Stephen Whitehouse from Daisy Street, Canton, was fatally injured by shrapnel while fire-watching at the Student's Union in Cardiff. He was the only university student to die in action in Cardiff during the war. His younger brother was the late Father Bernard Whitehouse who subsequently became administrator of St David's Roman Catholic Cathedral. He and Stephen had served Mass at St Mary and the Angels Church, Canton, on the morning of the fatal raid. A memorial plaque to Stephen was unveiled in 2001 at the Catholic Chaplaincy in Park Place. Five other people were killed on the same night as Stephen as a result of bombs falling on Lake Road, Willows Avenue and Senghennydd Road.

It was not that Wales was not defended against air attacks. At a St David's Day event in London on 1 March 1941 the Air Minister, Sir Archibald Sinclair, said that week by week the defences in and around Wales grew stronger. He said there were fifteen times more barrage balloons flying over Wales in the spring of 1941 than eight months earlier. There were also six times as many ack-ack guns in the

Father Patrick Creed. *(John O'Sullivan)*   Father Michael Murphy. *(John O'Sullivan)*

principality and the Royal Air Force was also keeping a watch on the skies over Wales. He reminded guests that the Welshman Lloyd George, who was Prime Minister during the First World War, had stated that Germany would allow only 6-foot-2 nations to stand in the ranks – but the world owed so much to the little 5-foot-5 nations. He obviously included Wales in this category.

When the siren sounded at 8.25 p.m. on 3 March it signalled the start of another major raid on Cardiff. Lansdowne Road School and Moorland Road School, at opposite ends of the city, were set on fire by incendiary bombs. But the chief target was the docks. High explosives fell on the north side of Roath Dock, destroying seven lines of railway and blowing up wagons carrying timber and pit props. A high-calibre bomb also hit Mountstuart Dry Dock, damaging buildings but missing ships. An incendiary bomb lodged in the entry gantry of Spillers Mill, causing dust explosions and seriously damaging plant and machinery. Houses in Hinton Street, Madoc Road and South Park Road were hit. Although there were no fatalities in these streets, a total of forty-six people died in Cardiff that night.

During this raid St David's Roman Catholic Cathedral in Charles Street was gutted by fire-bombs. Curates Father Patrick Creed and Father Michael Murphy were fire-watching when the incendiaries landed on the roof. Father Murphy went into the sacristy to get the key of the Tabernacle, which he handed to Father Creed. By this time the sanctuary was well alight but Father Creed dodged the

Above: King George VI and Queen Elizabeth at Currans ammunition factory, Cardiff, on 15 March 1941. *Below*: The royal couple leaving Currans.

flames to open the Tabernacle and collect the Blessed Sacrament, which he carried through the burning building. He was followed by a group of children from Newtown, Cardiff's Little Ireland, who had sought refuge in the cathedral when the raid started. Firefighters and local residents knelt in the street as Father Creed carried the Blessed Sacrament 400 yards to St David's Hall, which was used as a pro-cathedral for the next eighteen years. Father Creed, who was parish priest of St Teal's, Whitchurch, for forty-three years said before his death in January 2000: 'Don't make me out to be a hero, it was the little children who were the brave ones that night.' (The cathedral, which was originally opened in 1887, was rebuilt on the bomb site in Charles Street and opened and blessed by Archbishop Michael McGrath in 1959.)

King George VI and Queen Elizabeth came to the city on 19 March 1941 and also went to other bombed areas in South Wales to boost the morale of the people. In Cardiff the Queen presented the lord mayor with eight pairs of blankets to distribute to victims of the blitz. Among those who received a pair were Mr and Mrs John Howells, who were both in their mid-eighties. Their home in Craddock Street, Riverside, was destroyed in the January blitz. They were rehoused in Salisbury Road but this house was destroyed in a raid in March 1941. The couple had thirteen children. One of their sons lost his house in Neville Street in January 1941. The gift of blankets from the Queen included a card showing a girl sewing a Union flag 'for freedom'.

Prime Minister Winston Churchill was cheered through the streets of Cardiff and Swansea in April 1941 as he drove in an open-top car, smoking a cigar and giving his famous V-sign. In his broadcast to the nation that same month Churchill told of his visits to great cities and seaports that had been most heavily bombed, and to some of the places where the poorest people had got it worst. He continued:

I have come back not only reassured, but refreshed. To leave the offices in Whitehall with their ceaseless hum of activity and stress, and go out to the front, by which I mean the streets and wharves of London or Liverpool, Manchester, Cardiff, Swansea or Bristol, is like going out of a hothouse on to the bridge of a fighting ship. It is a tonic which I should recommend any who are suffering from fretfulness to take in strong doses when they have need of it. It is quite true that I have seen many painful scenes of havoc, and of fine buildings and acres of cottage homes blasted into rubble-heaps of ruin. But it is just in those very places where the malice of the savage enemy has done its worst, and where the ordeal of the men, women and children has been most severe, that I found their morale most high and splendid. Indeed, I felt encompassed by an exaltation of spirit in the people which seemed to lift mankind and its troubles above the level of material facts into that joyous serenity we think belongs to a better world than this. . . . The British nation is stirred and moved as it has never been at any time in its long, eventful, famous history, and it is no hackneyed trope of speech to say that they mean to conquer or to die. . . . This ordeal by fire has even in a certain sense exhilarated the manhood and womanhood of Britain. The sublime but also terrible and sombre experiences and emotions of the battlefield, which for centuries had been reserved for the soldiers and sailors, are now shared, for good or ill, by the entire population. All are proud to be under the fire of the enemy.

Among the places Churchill visited during his time in Cardiff was the Royal Infirmary, which had been damaged in a raid. The City Lodge – later renamed St David's Hospital – was also hit, as was Llandough Hospital, near Penarth. Llandough was the newest hospital in the area, having been built in the 1930s. It suffered more damage than any other hospital in Wales. Seven wards were put out of action, but fortunately there was not one fatal casualty. Members of the Women's Voluntary Service (WVS) drove patients to safety while soldiers based at Dinas Powys cleared the bomb damage. The Health Authority rewarded the troops with a pack of cigarettes each a day.

There was one bright note among the grim days and nights of bombing. A man named Hall from Flaxland Avenue, Cardiff, presented twenty-one budgerigars to the zoo at Victoria Park.

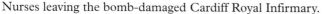

Nurses leaving the bomb-damaged Cardiff Royal Infirmary.

Mark Street, Riverside, where nine people were killed in a raid at the end of April 1941.

A NEW TYPE OF MINE

Two German bombers that targeted Cardiff on 30 April 1941 are believed to have been using a new type of parachute mine. Four of the deadly missiles caused widespread damage in Riverside and Cathays, more devastating than anything experienced in Cardiff up until that date. Houses crumbled into stone and dust. The civic buildings were almost certainly the main targets but the first mines fell at the rear of Coldstream Terrace in Riverside and in the castle grounds. An hour later two parachute mines landed in Llanblethian Gardens and Wyeverne Road.

At 19 Wyeverne Road, Philip and Emily Palmer and their eight children were all killed when a parachute mine fell in the back garden of their home. It landed just a few feet away from the Anderson shelter where Mrs Palmer and seven of the children were seeking refuge. Her husband and eldest son were killed while fire-watching nearby. Parts of the shelter were found the next day on the roof of a house in Rhymney Street.

This was a night when Civil Defence workers performed miracles. Families in Coldstream Terrace, Brook Street and Mark Street had sought refuge in the cellars of their homes and many were trapped. Men, women and children were buried in huge piles of debris in Wyeverne Road. Rescue workers toiled through the night

and the next day to reach the victims. Doctors crawled into the wreckage to administer morphine to the injured. More than 200 miners came down from the Rhondda to help in the work. Servicemen and women and members of the Home Guard were also involved.

The extent of the casualties and the damage was shocking. Some 33 people died in the raid and 56 were seriously injured; 54 houses were demolished by the mines, 328 were made uninhabitable, 1,484 were less seriously damaged and more than 500 had their windows blown out. The rescue work that night was described as one of Cardiff's finest hours.

That may have been true but not everything went to plan. More than 300 people had to be evacuated from their homes and according to Deputy Divisional Warden Alexander things went very wrong. He recorded: 'It is my sad duty to report that the evacuation was not handled satisfactorily.' He revealed that when 250 of the bombed-out people were sent to Gladstone Road School there was no one there to meet them. The wardens broke into the school and saved the day. Alexander said that the mix-up was discussed in secret as the authorities feared that news of it would affect the confidence and morale of the people. The right decision must have been taken, as there were no similar incidents in Cardiff during the war.

The Canton wardens, however, had a big disappointment when their cosy base at the Admiral Napier Hotel in Cowbridge Road East was considered unsuitable and they were transferred to a public shelter in Kitchener Gardens. It was a bitter blow to the wardens that they could no longer enjoy a pint of Brains Dark while on duty. A group of wardens at Curll Avenue kept themselves occupied between raids by forming a drama company and staging plays such as *Gaslight* at a variety of venues, including the Seamen's Mission, army camps and the Overseas Club in Charles Street. The plays were produced by Cyrus Rogers and the casts included Lillian Hopwood, A.W. Morgan, H.C. Williams, Mary Westcott and Gwen Player.

A variety of venues were used as bases for the ARP and fire-watchers but a row broke out in April 1941 when the lord mayor refused to allow the ARP to use the basement of the Mansion House in Richmond Road. He told the council that he might want to use the space himself.

The city's wardens and other rescue workers won great praise from the highest possible source. The Secretary of State for War, Herbert Morrison MP, travelled to Cardiff to see the organisations for himself. He told the City Council that Cardiff was unique among major cities in Britain for the way that its citizens had volunteered to act as wardens, fire-watchers and Civil Defence workers. He had a special word of thanks for the women carrying out key roles as ambulance drivers and members of the WVS.

But there was harsh criticism for people who jumped into their cars and drove away from Cardiff as German bombers came over. Members of the City Council's Air Raid Precautions Committee, which met in March 1941, passed one of the

Above left: Coldstream Terrace. *Left:* Prospect Drive, Fairwater.

Llanbleddian Gardens, Cathays, where twelve people were killed at the end of April 1941.

most extraordinary resolutions of the war. They decided to publish 5,000 posters with a message aimed at those who 'pack and run away, and have not got the guts to stay. If all were cowards such as you, my God, what would poor old England do?' Not all the council agreed with the strong wording of the poster. In the final version the word 'guts' was changed to 'pluck' and the last sentence was amended to read: 'Then, what would poor England do?'

The Air Raid Precautions Committee, under the chairmanship of Alderman Oswald Purnell, was far from happy with the watered-down version of the poster and officers were rapped over the knuckles for taking it to full council. They were also ordered to investigate how the so-call deserters obtained their petrol to do a runner. The committee also decided to buy 2,800 whistles for wardens – at a total cost of £70.

An indication of what life was like in Cardiff in the early days of the war can be found in the minutes of the city's Watch Committee, which controlled the police. Before every area of the city was fitted with sirens, special vans with loudspeakers toured the streets advising people to go to shelters. The chief constable was happy that the trams were taken off the road during air raids but he supported keeping the cinemas open – to close them would be bad for morale and could have caused panic, he said. But a committee recommendation to allow cinemas to open on a Sunday caused uproar. The Sunday showings would have been for service personnel and their partners only, but the scheme was dropped after objections from the Lord's Day Observance Society and the Council of Evangelic Churches.

There were no objections to Saturday and Tuesday night dances at the City Hall – admission 2s – with a Sergeant Pooler acting as master of ceremonies. One of the ten-piece bands was led by Garforth Mortimer, who was famous for his peacetime Sunday night concerts at the Park Hall. In 1922 Mortimer became the first musician in the world to make a broadcast. His violin recital from a room above Cardiff Market was broadcast to the Cory Hall, opposite Queen Street Station. An invited audience wore headphones to hear him play.

Mortimer's wartime concerts took place at around the time that a First World War veteran was donning her uniform again – the uniform of a tram conductress. In 1915 Edith Jones of Glenroy Street, Cardiff, was the first woman to work as a conductor in the city. In April 1941 she returned to the job to help keep the trams running. For the second time she became the first woman to sign up and she was appointed supervisor to the other women volunteers.

CIVIC CENTRE IN THEIR SIGHTS

On 2 May 1941 Reginald Charles, who won the Military Medal in the First World War, was killed in Cathedral Road. Nine days later, the Civic Centre was targeted again and a bomb hit Glamorgan County Hall, landing in the Treasurer's Office. The room was not occupied at the time but the blast caused considerable damage. A low-flying bomber, guided by a fire at the Carlton Restaurant in Queen Street, made a deliberate attack on the City Hall. The bomb hit the side of the GEC building, less than 100 yards away. Another bomb hit the University Hostel in Park Place. The following day a man was killed at Sloper Road and on 9 December another man died at Green Street, Ely.

The bomb that hit the Treasurer's Department at County Hall underlined the County Council's wisdom in making contingency plans to protect its records. In April 1941 the *South Wales Echo* reported that microfiche records were being made of important documents. A battery of four cameras had been set up and workers were turning over page after page of valuable records to ensure that copies would be available should the documents be destroyed in an air raid. The County Council, the City Council, the University of Wales and the Technical College all made photographic records. More than half a million photographs were stored on the special reels of film, measuring 7 inches by 2 inches, each capable of storing 6,400 shots. The dedicated team of eight young people carrying out the work at County Hall were brought in from London but all had connections with Wales. In charge of the project was Horace Hughes, a native of Montgomeryshire.

The *Echo* reported that the films would be buried in a secret location in the Welsh hills. In fact they were placed in a government-commandeered stone mine on the edge of Bath, where they remained until the 1980s. Glamorgan Archivist Susan Edwards said the records were mainly those of the Quarter Sessions. The few dozen films and the original documents are now in a strongroom at Glamorgan Record Office in Cardiff and can be consulted by the public.

There were a few more minor raids on Cardiff in 1941, but no fatalities were recorded. The owners of the Plaza Cinema, in North Road, Cardiff, were told to paint the building as the local residents feared that the shining white structure would prove a tempting target for the Germans. However, nothing was said about the white Portland stone of the civic buildings.

On 31 July 1942 an air-raid warden was killed in Cyncoed Road. The next serious attack was on 28 August. Six people were killed, including workers at Roath Power Station and the tram depot in Newport Road. Two people were also killed at Pantbach Road, Rhiwbina, that night. On 13 March 1943 a couple were killed in Woodville Road and a man died in Guildford Crescent. St Teilo's Catholic Church, Whitchurch, had a narrow escape on 10 May 1943 when a landmine fell just yards away on Glan-y-Nant Road, killing a fire-watcher, 74-year-old Richard Hopkins.

The extent of the air-raid wardens' role was illustrated in a report published by Cardiff-based Glamorgan County Council at the end of the war. The county spent a total of £1.4 million on the ARP service, all but £15,000 of which was funded by the government. More than 50,000 volunteer wardens, many of them veterans of the First World War, were recruited throughout the county.

Cecilia (sixty) and Thomas Turner (seventy-four), who were killed in York Street during the last raid.

In addition to shouting to householders to 'put that light out', the men, women and teenagers were in the front line of rescue work and caring for families bombed out from their homes. The wardens commandeered 358 church halls, chapel vestries and community buildings to use as rest centres and food stores, where more than 100 tons of tinned goods, such as Spam and dried eggs were kept. They distributed 45,000 blankets. 13,000 mattresses, 2,000 camp beds, 10,000 towels and as many nappies. The victims of bombing were also given 15,000 knives and forks and 10,000 dinner plates.

Backing the wardens in their work were more than 9,000 'angels of mercy' – all members of the WVS. They descended on the bombed areas, providing tea and sandwiches for rescue workers and feeding the victims of the blitz in rest centres. The authors of Bombers Over Wales accepted that official statistics were interesting for historic reasons but added, 'figures cannot measure the endurance shown by the wardens, WVS and other volunteers as well as the bomb victims during this grim period'.

Cardiff was one of the Royal Naval bases for the Western Approaches Command and the docks

St Agnes Road, where the last bomb fell. *Inset:* Ivy Pasley, her son Terry and the 'Superted' who survived the blast.

suffered air raids on seventeen occasions between 1940 and 1943. The city's Cathays cemetery has a total of 722 war graves. More than 200 Second World War victims are buried there, including airmen from St Athan and Cardiff air bases. Some 40 French and Norwegian casualties are also interred at Cathays.

LAST RAID TERROR

While other parts of Britain continued to be targeted by the Luftwaffe, Cardiff was relatively quiet – until the early hours of 18 May 1943. The raid was unexpected and vicious. It was the only time during the war that the Germans used their screaming Stuka bombers during a night raid on Britain.

The siren sounded at 2.36 a.m. and the all-clear signal came 83 minutes later at 3.59 a.m. During the raid sixty high explosives and parachute mines, and hundreds of incendiary bombs were dropped on the city killing forty-one people, seriously wounding fifty-two and slightly injuring seventy-six others.

The first incendiaries fell near Llanishen Reservoir. Then the German squadron, which had taken off from an airfield in occupied France, followed the railway line from Whitchurch, Rhiwbina and the Heath to Cardiff's Queen Street and Bute Street. Houses were struck in Pantbach Road, Llwynfedw Gardens and on the council housing estate at Mynachdy. The worst incident was in St Agnes Road at the Heath where a row of modern houses received a direct hit, killing or burying a number of people. But there was one remarkable rescue operation.

The home of the Pasley family in St Agnes Road was destroyed, but Mrs Ivy Pasley and her two-year-old son Terry were found alive. Mrs Pasley, who at the age of eighty-nine attended the sixtieth-anniversary memorial service of the raid at the City Hall, says they survived because of advice given to her by her husband, who had worked repairing homes in London after the blitz there: he had told her to shelter under a table placed next to a chimney breast. Terry's teddy bear was found 100 yards from their wrecked home. Until his death he used his Superted as a prop in Sunday School classes at Ararat Baptist Chapel, Whitchurch.

It was not the first time that Ivy Pasley had been in a bombing zone. In January 1941, when she was seven months pregnant with Terry, she was staying with her mother in Grangetown. She and her unborn baby sheltered under the stairs as incendiary bombs rained down on the Penarth Road area and high explosives fell on Grangetown.

Jim Davies saw action as a soldier in Korea, Malaysia and Oman – but his worst experience of the war was at his grandmother's house in the centre of Cardiff during the last air raid on the city. Jim, who was then fourteen, was staying with his grandmother at 28 Frederick Street when the house was hit by a high-explosive bomb. His three cousins, aged between four and fourteen, and his aunt were sitting just yards from him in the cellar and were all killed as the house was totally destroyed. Jim woke up at the Cardiff Royal Infirmary a few days later, his head wrapped in bandages and his body pitted with glass and stone splinters. He learnt that Nana Davies and his brother had also been brought out alive from the wreckage of the house. Just before the thirtieth anniversary of the raid, Jim was working as a security man at the Masonic Temple in Churchill Way, a few hundred yards away from where the bomb had hit his family's house. 'God only knows how I survived,' he said.

Cardiff-born singer and entertainer Two-Ton Tessie O'Shea was appearing at the city's New Theatre during the week of the last air raid. When I met her in Plantaganet Street, Riverside, in 1978 she told me how she had been staying with relatives there

Tessie O'Shea with a neighbour in Plantaganet Street where she stayed on the night of the last raid on Cardiff.

Cleaners who were charged with clearing Bute Street station after the raid in 1943.

when the raid started. She joined her neighbours in a communal shelter – and led a good old-fashioned sing-song. 'We were scared, but there was a great spirit,' she said.

Appearing on the same bill at the New Theatre that week were Victor Barnet and Alec Brook, two of the best table-tennis players in Britain. They entertained the audience with an exhibition of their skills. It was an appropriate act as the inventor of the bouncing bomb, Barnes Wallis, had used table-tennis balls to help him perfect the weapon which was dropped on the Ruhr dams the night before.

During the raid of 18 May 1943 the rescue services saved twenty-one people and recovered twenty-nine bodies from the rubble of their homes and shelters. A total of 4,300 houses and 140 shops were damaged. Bute Street station suffered considerable damage but the occupants of two nearby community shelters escaped with a few minor injuries. Two major fires broke out, one at Brown Brothers, a motorcycle dealers in Adam Street, and another at the Welsh Cold Stores, also known as the ice-house, in Pellet Street. Forty-five minor fires were reported.

A number of bombs were dropped on the railway line between Queen Street station and Cardiff General Hospital, and it was several days before normal train service was resumed. The choice of this target was not surprising because a bird's-eye view of the railway line was included in a book of potential targets issued to all German aircrews. Premises on the docks were also destroyed or damaged in the raid and nearly all the telephone lines to the docks were put out of action. This seriously affected the Admiralty Offices at Jackson Hall in Westgate Street.

Kühnemann's Nazi membership card recorded his links with Cardiff and Newport (O'Sullivan archives)

The raid was the seventeenth and last on Cardiff Docks. During the bombing the Guest Keen steelworks was hit for the first time during the war. Water was cut off from 441 houses, 2 churches and a nursing home, and supplies had to be provided by tankers.

As dawn broke a *Western Mail and Echo* reporter walked through the Heath and from a battered house in Rhydelig Avenue he heard a young married couple singing 'I'll Walk Beside You in the World Today'. The reporter described it as a message and a challenge.

The last two bombs, two parachute mines, fell at the junction of Maesycoed Road and Allensbank Road. The Germans were almost certainly targeting the American troops who were based at Heath Park or the Royal Ordnance Factory at Llanishen.

NAZIS WHO KNEW CARDIFF

Senior Air Raid Warden Gilbert Shepherd told the author of *Bombers Over Wales* that the last raid must have been planned by a Nazi who knew Cardiff. And that Nazi may have been Hans Henri Kühnemann, who was managing director of the German-owned Flottmann Drill Factory in Allensbank Road from 1935 until he fled Britain for Germany only 24 hours before war was declared on 3 September 1939. The factory was less than a mile away from the junction of Maesycoed Road and Allensbank Road, the spot where the last two parachute mines to fall on Cardiff were dropped.

Kühnemann, who was born in Cologne in 1900, joined the Nazi Party in 1932 and his Nazi membership card, issued on 1 January 1933 and now in the record office at Berlin, shows that he had knowledge of Newport and Cardiff. Kühnemann's office was in Allensbank Road, a site later occupied by a builders' yard. I discovered the link between the Nazi and the Flottmann company when

I reported on a strike at the factory in 1961. A manager was preparing for the company to be returned to its German owners. He said that before the war, on the wall behind Kühnemann's desk was a photograph of Adolf Hitler and a swastika flag. There was also a framed photograph of Kühnemann with Joachim von Ribbentrop, who was the German Ambassador to Britain in the 1930s and who was hanged for war crimes after the Nüremberg trials of leading Nazis.

Islwyn Evans, former press officer for the National Coal Board, was a reporter with the *South Wales Echo* in the 1930s and knew Kühnemann. He described the German engineer, who stood nearly 6½ feet tall as 'arrogant'. Kühnemann boasted in front of the reporter that he was sent from Germany as an industrial spy. The British Intelligence Service kept a close eye on him – MI5 and MI6 officers are said to have monitored his visits to the Midlands.

A few days before the outbreak of war the Kühnemanns and Flottmann's company secretary Herbert Steer and his wife went on a business trip to London but stayed at different hotels. Steer left his hotel on the day before war was declared and when he returned he told his wife that the Kühnemanns had fled the country with members of the German Embassy staff. They almost certainly went to Holyhead, from where they caught a boat that took them out into the Irish Sea where they boarded a German merchant ship. Mrs Steer told me in the 1960s that this came as a surprise because the Kühnemanns had told her they planned to stay in Britain in the event of war.

When war broke out the Flottmann company was taken over by the British government under the Custodian of Enemy Property Act. Herbert Steer, company secretary under Kühnemann, was placed in charge of the firm. Steer's widow told me that Kühnemann was proud of having been one of the first people to join the Nazi Party. He signed up in 1933. Kühnemann and his wife – reported to be the daughter of a Church of England clergyman – lived at 82 Marlborough Road, Cardiff. They had a butler, whom Kühnemann said would join him if he was ever taken to prison. Mrs Steer next heard from Kühnemann in the 1960s when he wrote to her from Germany. He asked for a reference from her husband to help the Kühnemanns to return to live in Britain, not knowing that Herbert Steer had died in 1959. Mrs Steer was so disgusted that she burnt the letter.

According to a report in the *South Wales Echo* in the 1950s Kühnemann had co-operated with the American Intelligence Service after the war. The *Echo* also reported that the Nazi had returned to Britain, but was recognised in a Pall Mall Club and jailed. The Home Office has no record of this.

'JARMANY CALLING'

Kühnemann was not the only Nazi connected with Cardiff. Dr Friederick Schoberth, who was Professor of German at Cardiff University from 1928 to 1939, joined the Nazi Party in Berlin in 1942. I interviewed him in Nüremberg in 1986, when he was terminally ill. He was in Germany on holiday when war broke out in

Above: Schoberth's Nazi membership card. *Above right*: Dr Friedrich Schoberth, Nüremberg, 1986. *Below*: Lord Haw-Haw after his arrest in 1945.

September 1939 and joined the Nazi Party three years later. He was on the staff of the German foreign office and his jobs included editing the scripts of the hated broadcaster Lord Haw-Haw, William Joyce, whose propaganda messages started with the infamous words, 'Jarmany Calling'.

Before the war, American-born William Joyce, who held both British and Irish passports, lived in Colum Road, Cardiff, and also in Newland Street, Barry. He was captured trying to flee Germany in 1945 and was hanged for treason in London in 1946. Con O'Sullivan of Beddau, Mid Glamorgan, was one of the British soldiers who looked after Joyce when he was arrested in Germany in 1945. According to him, Joyce lectured at a college in Cardiff, but I have found no evidence of this.

After the war Dr Schoberth spent 18 months in a British prison camp before a former Cardiff University colleague helped to secure his release. He returned to Nüremberg where he contributed to the rebuilding of the city's university, which had been destroyed in the blitz. When I asked Schoberth if he had helped plan any of the raids on Cardiff, he replied, 'Cardiff, my lovely Cardiff. How could I? My daughter is buried in Llanishen churchyard.' Schoberth and his wife came back to Cardiff in the 1950s to visit the grave of their daughter who died of meningitis in 1937 when she was only four. Her headstone can be seen in the cemetery.

It seems that when Schoberth was at Cardiff University in the 1930s there was considerable interest in all things German among some staff and students. A brief report in *Cap and Gown*, the university magazine, gives an insight:

The German Society reports that never has the society been more popular or more German. The first meeting of the academic year was crowded with students, members of the staff and Germans living in Cardiff. German folk songs, taught by Dr Schoberth, made the tone of the gathering highly Teutonic. Perhaps later the suggestion of the committee will be realised and beer and sausage will make the German Society still more German. The Society is going to give a play *Der Bestten* [*The Best*] at the end of term, while several coffee and chat evenings will be held where members of the society will tell why they go to Germany.

It seems no information survives about why Cardiff students wanted to go to a Germany led by Hitler and controlled by the Nazi Party. Dr Schoberth told me that he did go to prison while in Cardiff – to entertain the inmates with German folk songs.

Schoberth was not the only Welsh link with Lord Haw-Haw. One of the doctors who answered the call for help at the Senghenydd pit disaster, which caused 440 deaths in October 1913, was a Dr O'Sullivan, a family doctor from Ebbw Vale. In 1927 one of his two sons, Dr Florence O'Sullivan, a newly graduated GP, went underground to treat some of the injured in the Cwm Colliery disaster, which claimed more than fifty lives. In the 1960s Dr Florence revealed that he had been a classmate of William Joyce. The Ebbw Vale GP said he had seen a fight when another student at St Ignatius School in Ireland broke Joyce's nose. This injury resulted in the nasal problem that made the tone of Haw-Haw's 'Jarmany Calling' message so distinctive. Dr Florence also remembered the principal tutor at St Ignatius, a Father Baragrey, stating that Joyce would either be a genius or find himself at the end of a hangman's rope.

Because of his time in South Wales Joyce had a good knowledge of the area and he put it to use during his broadcasts. On one occasion he expressed sympathy with people queuing in the mud of Temperance Town, Cardiff, to catch an overcrowded Thomas's bus to Barry. (Temperance Town was an old part of Cardiff where the houses were demolished in the 1930s. It was not redeveloped until after the war when the city's bus station was built there.) Joyce knew all about Thomas's buses because, as he told Con O'Sullivan, the Welshman who was one of his jailers in 1945, he worked for Thomas Motors at Barry during the 1930s. In his broadcasts Haw-Haw also commented that the Town Hall clock at Barry was a minute faster on the dial facing Holton Road than the dial facing Central Park. He was right.

A priest who later joined the Cistercians at Caldey Island was one of the last people to see Joyce alive, and probably received the last letter that Haw-Haw wrote from the death cell. Before he died in the 1980s, Father Edmund spoke of his visits to Pentonville prison where he was chaplain and of an earlier letter in which Joyce told him he did not intend to seek re-admission to the church. But on the eve of the execution, Joyce made the Sign of the Cross and knelt for Father Edmund's blessing. A few hours later Joyce wrote to the priest: 'At the time of transition I shall have the immense help of your prayers. In the calmness of the grace, which He has given me, I shall think of your friendship until the last here and then beyond.' The letters were destroyed after Father Edmund's death at his request.

Joyce's body was later exhumed and taken to Galway, Ireland, for reburial.

DAM REVENGE?

In July 1943 a German spy was arrested in Marlborough Road, Cardiff. He was a Czechoslovakian working as a porter at Cardiff Royal Infirmary and he had been sending radio messages to Germany. He almost certainly told his controller that Guy Gibson had led 617 Squadron's Dam Busters raid on Germany on 16/17 May 1943, and that may be the reason why the city was targeted on 18 May, because Gibson had strong links with Cardiff. He was married to Eva Moore, an actress who lived in Penarth, and the couple spent time in South Wales during the war (see p. 91). Gibson was in Penarth when the news came through that he had been awarded the VC for his leadership of the raid and he celebrated at Penarth Golf Club.

The Dam Busters raid deployed the bouncing bomb invented by scientist Barnes Wallis and brought disaster to the Ruhr Valley as key dams were breached by 617 Squadron. More than 4,000 people were killed and 120,000 made homeless as the water rushed down the valley, destroying everything in its path. No. 617 Squadron trained for the raid over the reservoirs of the Elan Valley in Mid Wales.

It should be said that the Gibson connection is only one possible reason for the raid of 18 May. That night Cardiff was not properly protected. Many of the gunners had left to take part in a competition at Aldershot with other ack-ack crews from bases around the country. A report published in the *South Wales Echo* on 25 May said that the absence of ack-ack crews allowed the German aircraft to fly almost unopposed as they bombed the city. By an extraordinary coincidence

A workshop at the Royal Ordnance Factory. *(ROF Archives)*

General Sir Frederick Pile, the officer commanding Britain's ack-ack defence forces, was staying in the Cardiff area on the night of the raid and was able to see for himself the problems caused by the inadequate defence of the city.

As valid as this reason may be for the last raid on the city, I remain convinced that the motive of revenge for the Dam Busters raid is a more likely explanation for Cardiff's suffering that night. Ack-ack crews from other parts of the country were taking part in the competition at Aldershot, so why weren't other towns and cities, some more important than Cardiff, selected by the Germans?

The all-clear sounded at 3.59 a.m. on 18 May 1943 and this turned out to be the last raid on Cardiff, despite the important role the city played in the build-up to D-Day, 6 June 1944. Thousands of American troops and vital military equipment sailed from the city and other South Wales ports on the way to join the fighting in Normandy.

After the last bombs fell on Cardiff the city was involved in a new and urgent battle – against venereal disease. A special clinic was established at Cardiff Royal Infirmary and lectures were held at factories and to members of the armed forces. The police were given powers to compel suspected victims to seek medical treatment.

FRIENDLY-FIRE VICTIMS

Sadly the raid on 18 May 1943 was not the last tragedy of the war in Cardiff. On 27 March 1944 there was a so-called friendly-fire incident when a stray shell from an ack-ack unit at Gabalfa hit a workshop at the Royal Ordnance Factory at Llanishen. It killed one man, his daughter and seven other women on the night shift. The factory, which had played a vital part in making ammunition and other military material, had escaped serious damage throughout the war only to suffer this loss of life.

One of the women injured in the incident was Doris Tanner, who wrote to me on the fiftieth anniversary of the raid in 1994. She said:

Above: ROF staff at a Workers' Playtime Concert. *Below:* A group of women who worked at the ROF during the war. *(ROF Archives)*

It was queer what happened, I can't remember hearing any explosion. It seemed as if everything went dark and I felt myself floating to the ground. I don't remember feeling any pain at the time and I was aware of everything around me. There was a lot of noise and the air was full of steam. It was like mist around. The first-aiders were soon among us and we were put on stretchers. The nurse was great and worked well, but a doctor tore her off a strip because of the shortage of morphine in the surgery.

I was taken to the City Lodge [later named St David's Hospital] where a day room had been turned into a ward for four of us girls who had been injured. I was there until the middle of June when the beds were needed for troops injured in the D-Day invasion.

When I was attending Llandough Hospital for treatment to my injured hand I met an ATS woman. She told me she was on the gun that had fired the rogue shell. She said that the gun was in Western Avenue and when the shell left the weapon the gun crew knew straight away that something was wrong. She was so sorry that they had done what the Germans had failed to do – hit the ROF factory.

The late Nancy Davies of Cardiff said she and other workers at the factory had continued to work throughout the air raids, making military supplies. They never sought refuge in a shelter. A supermarket now stands on the site of the friendly-fire incident. Ironically its name is Safeway.

CELEBRATIONS

Cardiff celebrated VE Day in style on 8 May 1945. Rations were pooled to cater for street parties, and people danced and sang throughout the day and night. Local solicitor Charles Hallinan went before the magistrates and successfully applied for late-night licences for the pubs. But he sounded a sober note for the justices. 'Supplies of beer and spirits are still low and there is no guarantee that there will be enough to serve all those who are celebrating,' he said.

A memorial service and victory parade was held in Cardiff on the first Sunday after the cessation of hostilities. The service at St John the Baptist Church was conducted by the Revd J.A. Lewis and the sermon was preached by the Bishop of Llandaff. Places were reserved for people bereaved during the blitz. After the service, the Duke of Beaufort, representing King George VI, took the salute outside the City Hall. The Lord Lieutenant, Sir Gerald Bruce, regarded the occasion as the moment when the people of Cardiff could cheer their defenders until none of the bands could be heard. Representatives of most of the organisations who had been involved in rescue work and caring for those made homeless or injured during the blitz were invited – but for some reason there was no official invitation to members of the Home Guard.

A crowd outside the New Theatre, Cardiff, on VE Day.

Many of the victims of the blitz in South Wales are buried in unmarked graves. There is no major monument to the men, women and children who died as a result of enemy bombing, but when Ricky Ormonde was Lord Mayor in the mid-1990s, he erected a memorial to fifty-one of the victims who are buried in Cathays Cemetery, Cardiff. The cemetery was closed for three weeks after the raid of 18 May 1943 because of damage caused to the area by parachute mines. American troops stationed at Heath Park helped in the clear-up. It was during this time that a boxing glove in a glass cover disappeared from the grave of Peerless Jim Driscoll, the Cardiff boxer who gave up the chance of becoming a world champion to return to the city to fight an exhibition bout to raise money for Nazareth House orphans. When he died in 1925 the Sisters of Nazareth raised a Celtic cross headstone, which wrongly describes Peerless Jim as Flyweight Champion of the World.

In the 1960s town planner Professor Colin Buchanan put forward proposals that would have been more devastating to the cemetery than the German bombs. He suggested that a new road, known as the Hook Road, be carved through it. Had the plan gone ahead it would have meant exhuming 30,000 bodies from 10,000 graves and reburying them elsewhere. The plan was defeated by just one vote, four days after Labour candidate Yvette Roblin won a by-election in the true blue Cyncoed Ward after fighting on just one issue – stop the Hook Road.

No Mercy for Swansea

Swansea has one of the finest shopping centres in Britain, rebuilt after the Second World War during which the heart of the town was reduced to rubble. Most of the destruction occurred during three nights in February 1941 when scores of German bombers from airfields in occupied France dropped thousands of tons of explosives on targets marked by incendiaries. Most of the raiders flew over Lundy Island and approached Swansea via Worms Head. More raiders approached from the east. But the February raids were not the first suffered by the town.

The first casualties came on 10 July 1940 when eleven workmen were killed and more than thirty seriously injured at Swansea Docks. This attack came 24 hours after Cardiff suffered its first casualties when seven men died at the city's docks. The first big attack on Swansea was on 1 September 1940 when thirty-three people were killed, most of them in the Fisher Street area. This was the first major raid on Britain, the overture to the Battle of Britain and a forerunner of the London blitz later that month. The Nazis added to the terror in Swansea when they machine-gunned rescue workers on the ground. But there was praise for one of the German aircrews from author and publisher Victor Gollancz in a book printed after the war that illustrates acts of mercy by some of the enemy. Gollancz told of how one Swansea man got caught on barbed wire while dodging the machine-gun bullets. He was a sitting target, but the German pilot saw his plight and stopped firing at him.

The Swansea raid of 1 September 1940 resulted in the award of one of the first George Medals of the war. It went to 27-year-old fitter and turner William Jenkins of Stepney Street, Cwmbwrla. He was a motorcycle messenger and the citation described his perilous journey from the ARP base at Manselton to the control room in the Guildhall. It told how he dodged falling debris and burst gas mains and continued:

In Trinity Place he was knocked off his machine by falling bricks and although temporarily knocked out managed to get going again. Near the Institute for the Blind in Northampton Place he was blown off his motorcycle by an exploding bomb and again rendered unconscious. He was taken to a shelter but when he came round he insisted on continuing his journey, only to be again knocked unconscious by another bomb blast. In a bedraggled state, he finished the last half-mile on deflated tyres. He was suffering from shock but his only apparent injury was a splinter in his thumb. After delivering the important message he refused to be taken home by car and reported back for duty at the ARP centre.

George Medal winner William Jenkins.

For his leadership of wardens in the same raid, Haydn Hughes of Caswell Road, Mumbles, was commended in dispatches.

THREE NIGHTS OF TERROR

The September raid was devastating but the death toll was even higher on 18 and 19 January 1941 when fifty-five people were killed.

The Imperial War Museum has a fascinating relic of the January raids, a 1,400kg bomb, which was dropped during the night of the 17th/18th in the Swansea Docks area but failed to explode. Martin Garnet, a weapons expert at the museum, said that the bomb passed through a full 10-ton coal truck, the truck's 4½-inch steel axle and a rail before penetrating the ground to a depth of 25 feet. In doing so it swerved first to the right, then to the left, and finally upwards before coming to rest 14 feet below the surface and about 35 yards from the point of entry. It was recovered by Royal Navy personnel after ten weeks' work during a period of gales, rain and snow. They had to excavate to a total depth of 54 feet, and the pit they were working in became flooded.

However, Swansea's worst ordeal was still to come. The town was under constant attack for three nights, 19, 20 and 21 February 1941. A total of 227 people died during those 72 hours – 122 men, 68 women and 37 children under the age of 16. A further 254 people were seriously injured and 137 slightly injured. The teenage victims included a number of young ARP messengers and fire-watchers, some of them still at school.

The town centre, including the market, was wiped off the map. The area from Castle Street to the corner of Union Street and Oxford Street was laid waste. A total of 282 houses were completely destroyed and 11,084 were damaged but considered repairable. Extensive damage was caused on the Mayhill and Townhill housing estates and in the suburbs of Brynmill, Manselton, Brynhyfryd, Mount Pleasant and St Thomas. Some 395 shops, 107 offices and 82 industrial buildings were completely gutted. Schools completely destroyed or badly damaged included

Bomb-damaged St Mary's Church, Swansea.

Brynhyfryd, Brynmill, Cwm, Danycraig, Dyfatty, Hafod, Plasmarl, St Thomas, St Joseph's Nursery, the Grammar School for Boys, Dynevor Secondary School for Boys, De La Beche Secondary School for Girls, Glanmor Secondary School for Boys and the Technical College. The BBC studios in Alexandra Road were levelled, as were the Food Control Centre in Rutland Street and the town's abattoirs. Two high-explosive bombs fell near the new civic centre but caused only superficial damage.

The raiders didn't spare churches and among those destroyed was Swansea's mother church of St Mary's, part of which dated back to 1621. It has been rebuilt and the story of the blitz is told in its stained-glass windows. Holy Trinity, St Philip's, Wesley Chapel, Capel Gomer, Mount Pleasant Chapel, Alexandra Road Chapel, Pell Street Chapel, Zoar Chapel, St Joseph's Priory, St Andrew's, Carmarthen Road Chapel, Ebenezer Chapel, the Forward Movement Hall, St Mathew's, St Thomas's and the Jewish synagogue were all either destroyed or severely damaged.

Patients had to be transferred from the General Eye Hospital while bombs rained on the area. Also damaged were Trinity Place Clinic, Rhianfa Maternity Home and Graig House Hospital. Picton House Cinema was burnt out, while the Albert Hall and the Empire were affected but less seriously.

Traffic ground to a halt as roads were closed because of debris or unexploded bombs. More than a hundred massive craters added to the chaos in eighty streets. Sewers, gas mains and electricity supplies were put out of action. Nearly sixty water mains were smashed, including the one that supplied the Townhill area. Forty-four of the pipes were repaired within a fortnight but residents in large parts of the town had to queue for rationed supplies. The shortage of water also hindered the firefighters, who were faced with their biggest ever challenge. There were vain attempts by some householders to save their properties by using stirrup pumps.

Contemporary reports tell how by the third day, a Friday, the whole town appeared to be on fire. The merciless raiders continued to drop heavy bombs into the flames. Hundreds of people were evacuated from their homes because of unexploded bombs. It is estimated that 800 heavy explosives were dropped during the three days and of these only 66 failed to explode. Thousands of incendiaries fell all over the town; many were tackled by ordinary people using the contents of sandbags. Courageous Civil Defence teams had problems coping after three days without sleep and the town found it difficult to deal with the accumulating problems.

BASKETS OF ONIONS

There was a thin blanket of snow on the ground when the Germans dropped their first bombs around 7 p.m. on Wednesday 19 February. The attack lasted for 5 hours and similar raids took place on the Thursday and the Friday. The first aircraft dropped flares over Swansea Bay, lighting up the town and making it easy

The main shopping centre in Swansea was reduced to rubble in February 1941.

for the German Luftwaffe to find targets. The flares, nicknamed baskets of onions, hovered over the town as incendiary bombs followed by high explosives were dropped almost non-stop.

One of the saddest incidents was at 16 Mayhill Road. Constance Camden, aged thirty-seven, her daughters Constance (eleven) and Judith (five), and son Wallace (fifteen), an ARP messenger, were all killed when their house took a direct hit. The news was broken to Constance's husband who was serving in the Royal Army Medical Corps.

It was on the Friday night that most of the damage to the town centre was caused. Major fires broke out and acted as beacons for more deadly bombs from the raiders, which targeted the town centre and the nearby hills. The area from Castle Street to Oxford Street appeared to be one mass of flames. The glow above the town convinced people on the English side of the Bristol Channel that Swansea had been destroyed in a great inferno.

Fred Martin, the landlord of the Duke Hotel, cut hundreds of sandwiches to feed the firemen and rescue workers. He even found time to tackle a blaze that broke out in the back of his own premises.

Ben Evans's store in Wind Street was quickly burnt out while Oxford Street was a continuous line of fire, too hot for firemen to get anywhere near the scene. Fire-fighters from many South Wales towns headed for Swansea to give what help they could. As dawn broke the full human tragedy was evident. Families who had lost their homes were wandering around what was left of the streets, holding pathetic bundles of belongings and looking for rest centres in buildings that were still standing.

When the three days of hell were over the inquest began into what had happened. Questions were asked about why Swansea had fewer guns to protect it than Cardiff and other parts of Britain. There was also a mystery over why the guns were silent on the last night of the attack. One suggestion was that there were plans for British fighter planes to take on the Luftwaffe and there were fears that the ack-ack crews might shoot down one of their own aircraft. Whatever the case, British planes did not put in an appearance and the Germans had a free run to attack Swansea.

Experts analysing the raid decided that the Germans had used a new tactic. In previous raids on Britain the pattern was to drop hundreds of incendiaries followed by tons of high explosives. When Swansea was attacked the incendiaries and high explosives were dropped by alternate waves of enemy aircraft. This successful method was subsequently adopted throughout the war.

AFTERMATH

After the raid Swansea MP William Mabane, who was Parliamentary Secretary to the Minister of Home Security, described the mood of the people as angry, but not depressed. Chief Constable Frank Joseph May, in an official report, said there had been a stiffening of the upper lip and a determination to 'pay the Hun back'. The borough electrical engineer, a man called Blackstone, peppered his thoughts with a mass of clichés. He said that Swansea people 'wanted an eye for an eye and a tooth for a tooth' and were 'determined not to turn the other cheek'.

The Town Clerk and Chief Controller, H. Lang Coath, who was awarded the CBE for his leadership, gave this graphic description of the Saturday after the three-day attack:

We found roads impassable. Fifteen schools had been destroyed or severely damaged; telephones cut off; a casualty list, providentially not so large as might be expected (227 people died and 254 were seriously injured. Over 6,537 people without a home.) The post office completely demolished and all papers, books and records, including thousands of food registrations, destroyed. The shopping centre, including the market, wiped out. A total of 171 food shops destroyed, 64 grocers, 61 butchers, 12 bakers, and 34 hotels,

The remains of Ben Evans's store, Wind Street, Swansea.

restaurants, and cafés. Gas and water cut off causing cooking problems for those homes still standing.

Dangerous buildings required immediate attention; the blitz area had to be cordoned off, rescue work had to go on, the dead had to be identified and buried. It just needed a match to cause panic and consternation and to put everything in hopeless muddle and disorder.

The town clerk revealed that more than 8,000 messages and 561 incidents had been logged at the ARP control room during the three nights of raids.

The problem of feeding the homeless was tackled with the help of sixteen mobile canteens, which were dispatched from the War Room at the City Hall in Cardiff.

H. Lang Coath was full of praise for the ARP and other Civil Defence workers, especially his right-hand man, ARP Officer Brayley. Sixty-one rest centres were set up in the town. Two special cafés were opened, providing 2,000 meals a day. Twenty-two water tankers were brought into the borough to distribute supplies over a wide area. The mayor was given a fund of £50,000 to help families overcome immediate financial problems.

The town clerk told of the devotion and heroism of people who seemed to have been brought closer together by a common peril. All were neighbours, there were no strangers within Swansea's battered gates. In every street there were acts of gallantry in firefighting and rescue work. In his report he added, 'Swansea was scarred and stricken but its spirit shone throughout with a glorious light challenging the fury of the flames which destroyed the town centre.'

ACTS OF BRAVERY

There were many acts of bravery during the February raids, one of the most remarkable at the premises of the Swansea Gas Light Company. The story was related at the time by company manager W.H. Jones:

A shower of incendiaries fell in the storage and distributive part of the works. Workers quickly dealt with the fire-bombs which were accessible, but it was noticed that a growing flame which was then curling five feet into the air was issuing from the Number Four gas holder crown, presenting a target and threatening the whole of the gas works. The holder contained 67 feet of gas and a ladder had to be used to reach the seat of the fire.

Lorry driver George Peters and foreman John Thompson climbed a ladder to the girder of the burning holder, drawing a second ladder with them. Thompson straddled the girder while Peters climbed to the crown of the holder. Incendiaries and high explosives were still falling in the vicinity but the men succeeded in getting the fire under control and prevented what might have been a calamity.

George Peters was awarded the George Medal, John Thompson was made a member of the Order of the British Empire and E.J. Forward, a watchman on the site, was commended for brave conduct.

The leader of the 24th Swansea (Wesley) Scout Troop was awarded the Scouts' Bronze Cross – the Scouts' equivalent of the VC – for his gallantry. As the bombs fell, King's Scout Jack Evans, who was nineteen, manned the telephone at a bomb-damaged ARP post and helped to maintain vital communications. On the second night he was again on duty in an area that was savagely bombed. He tackled incendiaries, salvaged furniture, helped in rescue work and gave first aid to the injured. A senior warden was killed alongside him but Jack escorted women and children from burning buildings among bursting bombs. His official citation read: 'Although in continuous danger of his life, knowing the risks and viewing the horror, he remained on duty for three nights.'

Even greater praise was poured on him by an organiser of a firefighting team: 'Jack Evans had the strength of ten men, encouraging the people all the time, acting as an inspiration to all. He saved one house and probably many others (he used water from cisterns to douse the flames). The Boy Scouts are to be thanked for turning out such citizens.'

Three air-raid wardens and three messengers were killed during the February raids. Four other rescue workers also died. Three firemen, including two from Pontardawe, were killed and thirty-four were injured, eight of them seriously, as brigades tackled a total of 192 fires.

PHOSPHOROUS BOMBS

The next major raid on Swansea took place on the night of 16 February 1943, almost two years to the day since the Germans had virtually destroyed the town. The districts of Mount Pleasant and St Helens suffered most in the 1943 raid when 34 people were killed, 61 seriously injured and 50 slightly hurt. Some 82 high explosives, 750 phosphorous bombs and 2,000 incendiaries were scattered over a wide area; 40 buildings were demolished and 850 houses were damaged but repairable. By this time Swansea was guarded by British aircraft, which prevented the bombers reaching military targets in the area.

The Griffiths, Thomas and Folland Wards at the General Hospital in St Helen's Square were destroyed and the roof and windows damaged. A decision was taken to evacuate 300 patients because there was an unexploded high-explosive bomb on the Phillips Parade side of the building. Doctors and nurses moved the patients through piles of debris, with no lighting and with the added danger of escaping gas. Only one patient died during the evacuation. The matron, Miss E.A. Smith, and the hospital secretary O.C. Howells, were praised for their leadership.

Children and the elderly and infirm had to be evacuated that night from Tawe Lodge after a bomb destroyed nearby houses. Young probationer nurses, returning from a dance in the town, went to the aid of the children in the isolation block.

They found that the blast had torn open pillowcases and covered the ward and the children with hundreds of feathers.

One hero of the blitz was deeply mourned by the people of Swansea after that raid. He was Devonian Lieutenant Edward James Douglas, holder of the Military Medal. He was a member of the Royal Engineers bomb disposal squad and he lost his life dealing with an unexploded bomb in Hospital Square. He had dealt with many unexploded bombs in the area and given lectures to other services. He was a Freeman of the City of London and the son of Tregarthen and Ada Douglas. His wife Muriel lived in London. Lieutenant Douglas is buried in St Petrox Churchyard, Dartmouth.

Police War Reservist Hadyn Powell was partly blinded by a bomb splinter near the General Hospital but this did not stop his going to the aid of two mortally injured soldiers lying on the pavement. He stayed at his post despite his injuries, which included wounds to his face, chest and legs. He was mentioned in dispatches for his devotion to duty.

DEFYING DANGER

Scores of unexploded bombs fell on South Wales during the blitz and were dealt with by teams of Royal Engineers who risked their lives every time they tackled one of the dangerous monsters. In the front line of that work was Londoner Colonel Stuart Archer, now chairman of the Victoria Cross and George Cross Association and President of the Royal Engineers Bomb Disposal Branch. He was awarded the George Cross for dealing with unexploded bombs in Swansea on 2 September 1940 when a vast fire started in six oil tanks in a raid on the National Oil Refineries at Skewen. There were eleven unexploded bombs in and around the oil tank farm and Archer, then a lieutenant, led the team that went to work 8 hours after the

A bomb disposal squad at work, Swansea.

Prime Minister Winston Churchill came on a morale-boosting trip to Swansea in 1941. Here he meets nurses at Swansea Hospital. *(Imperial War Museum)*

raid. Three bombs exploded belatedly, but this did not deter Archer's team from the job in hand. One 250kg unexploded bomb had fallen 2 feet from the side of an oil tank. The fuse was ticking and could have gone off at any moment. Lieutenant Archer got rid of the filler cap, scraped away the explosive and removed the ticking fuse, which had sheared on impact. The fuse was needed by the War Office so Archer removed it by hand and found that the Germans had fitted it with an anti-handling device, which fortunately did not function. He removed this too and sent it off to the back-room scientists. It was the first such device to be salvaged successfully. Three more times Lieutenant Archer drove lorries carrying unexploded high explosives to isolated sites.

In the citation, which was published in the *London Gazette* on 30 September 1941, the inspector of fortification and director of bomb disposal paid tribute to Archer's deliberate and sustained courage, and said his devotion to duty was of the highest order.

The Swansea incident was one of many heroic deeds carried out by this man, who was an architect before joining the Honourable Artillery Company as a private solder at the age of twenty-three in 1938. He later transferred to the Royal Engineers and from 1940 was involved in bomb disposal work in South Wales. He not only defused or removed unexploded high explosives, but also extracted many fuses from the missiles, providing British scientists with valuable information about German bombs.

Lieutenant Archer dealt with more than 200 unexploded bombs. On 15 July 1940, four 250kg explosives were dropped on RAF St Athan. Two that failed to detonate landed only 10 yards away from important assembly sheds and could not be dealt with in situ. Lieutenant Archer's team, which was based in Cardiff, excavated the first bomb, knowing that it might be booby-trapped. It was loaded onto a lorry, which Archer drove to an isolated spot 2 miles away, where it was blown up without causing any damage. The same procedure was then carried out with the second bomb.

On 17 August 1940 in the village of Moulton in the Vale of Glamorgan – not far from the popular Three Horse Shoes pub – a 250kg bomb was excavated as far as the fuse pocket. It contained a No. 50 fuse, on which the War Office needed to experiment. An attempt was made to withdraw the fuse with a piece of cord and when this failed Stuart Archer released it by hand, using a pickhead. Ten days later Archer removed another fuse from an unexploded bomb at Port Talbot Docks, again providing vital information for the boffins.

By the end of the war the man who joined the army as a private was a major commanding 12 Bomb Disposal Company. After being demobbed in 1946 he returned to his wife Kit, whom he had married just six months before war was declared. He rejoined the army in 1950 before eventually returning to his civilian life as an architect. He was given the honorary rank of colonel in 1963. This brave, almost foolhardy, man to whom South Wales and particularly Swansea owes a great debt, succeeded Rear Admiral Godfrey Place VC as chairman of the Victoria Cross and George Cross Association in August 1994.

DOCKS BOMBED

There is no doubt that the Luftwaffe's interest in Swansea was focused on the docks, but in fact the port area escaped with comparatively little damage.

The first attack on the docks came on 27 June 1940 when a lone raider flew inland from Swansea Bay and dropped a string of bombs from the beach to Kilvey Hill. They missed the key target of the King's Lock. None of the bombs exploded and the only damage was to a house in Danygraig Road, where a missile penetrated two floors.

Death came to the docks for the first time on 10 July 1940. Eleven men working on the mole at the King's Dock were killed and thirty-five severely injured when a raider bombed the area. Ironically, minutes before the men had been waving at the pilot, believing the low-flying aircraft was a friendly one. This is not surprising as the Germans had captured the plane from the French. Most of the victims worked for the Great Western Railway Company. Ships berthed at the docks escaped damage in the raid, which came the day after Cardiff suffered its first fatal casualties, seven men unloading a ship there.

More bombs fell on Swansea's port area on 18 and 27 July that year. One hit the breakwater at the Queen's Dock, leaving 60 feet of the permanent way without

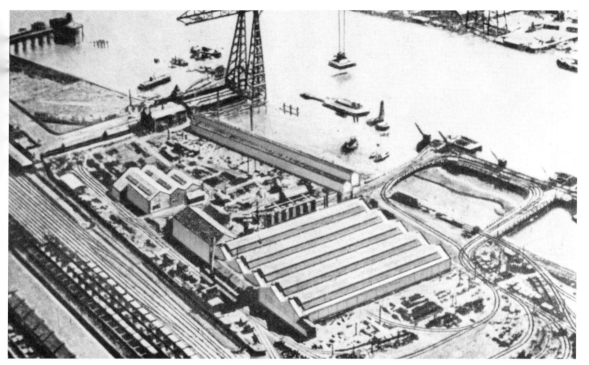

Swansea Docks, from a German guidebook.

foundations. Incendiaries rained on the docks on 1 September and a fisheries shed was gutted by fire. A high-explosive bomb landed near the harbour offices and demolished four buildings. A French submarine was holed in several places by shrapnel from bombs landing nearby. On 24 September 1940 an incendiary bomb fell on the office of the harbour manager, but was quickly dealt with.

Incendiaries also caused considerable damage to the port on 17 January 1941. A number of buildings were gutted, including the G and L sheds at the Prince of Wales Docks. High-explosive bombs wrecked three cranes and ripped up railway lines. Surprisingly, the docks were hardly touched during the three nights of raids on Swansea during February 1941, and this did not say much for the navigational and bombing skills of the Luftwaffe.

The only vessel to be sunk at Swansea during the Second World War was a tug in the King's Dock. Divers later discovered that it had not been holed and a heavy explosive bomb probably blasted it.

PRISON DAMAGED

Information is scarce about Swansea Prison during the war, although its location in Oystermouth Road was close to where some high explosives fell. The prison's historian Peter J.R. Goodall, a prison officer for more than twenty years, said it appears that the jail was used for internment purposes during hostilities. It housed

King George VI and Queen Elizabeth visited Swansea in March 1941.

a number of sailors from the docks who were arrested at the outbreak of war. The men's nationalities are not clear, but they were from countries friendly to Germany. There is no record as to how the prisoners coped during the raids or whether they were kept in their cells. Peter Goodall said that a survey carried out in the 1990s revealed evidence of bomb blast damage to some of the prison buildings.

Goodall's main contribution to the history of the prison is his book *For Whom The Bell Tolls* (Gomer, 2001). It is an account of executions carried out in Swansea during the twentieth century. No one was hanged at the prison between 1939 and 1945, but there was an execution during the First World War. Dan Sullivan was hanged in 1916 for the murder of his wife.

Raids on Newport

Newport did not suffer a major blitz, but fifty-one people were killed and sixty-six seriously injured in raids on the town. The first sirens sounded in Newport at 12.48 a.m. on 25 June 1940 and the following night a lone plane suddenly swooped over and dropped a stick of bombs, one of which set fire to an oil tank. Mr Riley, manager of the oil depot, stopped the fire spreading by risking his life to climb to the top of an adjoining tank to disconnect the link.

In September 1940 Emrys Jones, aged eighteen, a member of the Home Guard, was awarded the Military Medal for his brave attempt to rescue a workman, Stanley Jones, who died on the way to hospital.

On 13 September a German bomber crashed on the house of Mr and Mrs Harold Phillips at Stow Park Avenue, killing their two children. Seventeen-year-old Malcolm Phillips died a hero in an unsuccessful attempt to save his sister Myrtle, who was fourteen. The bomber struck the dining-room, which was on the ground floor, setting the property on fire. Malcolm and his parents were sleeping upstairs. His mother and father escaped by climbing to the ground by using knotted sheets, but the teenager dashed downstairs to try to reach his sister. They both perished in the flames. The plane that had dropped the bombs crashed after hitting the cable of a barrage balloon and the German pilot parachuted to safety.

Regrettably Malcolm was not posthumously recognised for his heroic attempt to rescue his sister, but the teenagers are remembered in a unique way. In the staff department at Newport Central Library there is a cabinet of children's books which were presented by the local Jewish community in memory of Malcolm and Myrtle. Part of the inscription is in Hebrew.

DIRECT HIT

On 10 October 1940 bombs fell in Lewis Street, Capel Street, Albion Street, Baldwin Street and Pottery Terrace. There was a direct hit on the Alexandra Dock Hotel in Watch House Parade. Three people were killed and others were trapped in the darts room. For their rescue efforts, Detective Constable Cook was awarded a George Medal, PC Wetter received the British Empire Medal, and Inspector Everson was commended.

Newport's former town clerk, Harold Griffiths, who was a past president of Newport Rotary Club, and his eighteen-year-old daughter Patricia died when a bomb hit their house in Fields Park Avenue.

Above: Eighteen-year-old Emrys Jones, who was in the Home Guard, was awarded the Military Medal for his brave attempt to rescue his workmate Stanley Jones, who died in hospital.

Left: George Medal winner Detective Constable Cook whose bravery at the Alexandra Hotel, Newport, gained him the award.

Newport fire-watchers included Scouts and senior citizens.

Parachute mines fell on Newport for the first time on 1 July 1941, and hundreds of people were evacuated from their homes in the Pill area after two of the monsters failed to explode. It was Newport's worst night of the war, with a total of thirty-seven people killed.

Thirty people in Eveswell Street were killed by just one bomb. Another crashed on a house in Kensington Place, killing eighty-year-old Alfred Searle, the doyen of Newport solicitors, and his housekeeper. Their remains were never found. After the war the grounds were turned into a park.

Workmen at Lysaghts held a mass meeting on the Sunday following the raid and passed a resolution praising the splendid way in which the authorities had coped with the emergency. Special mention was made of the persistent heroism of J.H. Huelin, although his brave deeds were not listed.

Wartime censorship prevented the *South Wales Argus* from reporting the raid. The newspaper was able only to describe the event as an attack on 'a South Wales town', but it did carry news of the first air raid on Moscow, which coincided with the bombing of Newport. A few days later the *Argus* carried obituaries of people who had died as a result of enemy action, but no addresses were printed and neither was the date of death. Censors feared such information would help the Germans.

Writing in the *Argus* on 1 July 1971, the thirtieth anniversary of the raid, journalist Lyndon Troy said that eight parachute mines fell across Newport from west to east that night. The first fell near Tredegar Park; others landed at Belle Vue

Park, Eveswell Street, Kensington Place, Beechwood Road and a field off Christchurch Road. Two more landed in the River Usk not far from the historic transporter bridge. Troy interviewed retired police inspector Slocombe, who had been on duty on the night of the raid. He told how the parachute mines exploded on contact with anything solid and the resulting blast caused considerable damage. An inquest was held to pronounce the deaths of six people whose remains were never found or could not be identified. A civic funeral was held for the six, with a service conducted by the Bishop of Monmouth. Mourners were led by the mayor of Newport and Sea Cadets formed a guard of honour.

In his 1971 report Lyndon Troy suggested that Newport was targeted in error and that the parachute mines were intended for Cardiff or the shipping lanes in the Bristol Channel. The Germans themselves reported Cardiff city centre had been attacked that night, but in fact the nearest they got was St Mellons.

After the raid Newport Council debated the possibility of constructing shelters carved out of hillsides to provide cover for every man, woman and child in the town. The motion was defeated by just thirteen votes to ten. Alderman E.W. Rowthorne, a former police superintendent, revealed that the Germans had dropped leaflets containing an extract from one of Hitler's speeches. Rowlands had sold some in aid of the town's Spitfire fund. Schoolboys collected their own relics, either bits of shrapnel from the ack-ack guns or pieces of cloth from the parachutes that landed the mines.

Rogerstone was a constant target throughout the war and the most serious damage was done on the evening of 7 October 1941. Two parachute mines fell on the village, one dropping harmlessly in a field, the other landing in the middle of Park Avenue, destroying a number of houses. Eleven people were killed and fifteen suffered serious injury.

Eleven people died when a landmine destroyed part of Rogerstone in October 1941.

Rogerstone residents surveying the damage.

An insight into the problems facing local authorities in wartime was outlined in a paper presented by Newport's chief sanitary inspector, Charles Burr, in June 1939. He said:

> We are accustomed to the gentle flow of circulars which normally emanate from government departments, but air raid precaution circulars and memoranda have fluttered down upon us like autumn leaves.
>
> Experience has shown that the only way to keep abreast of the circulars is to institute a first-class filing and indexing system and to place it in charge of a clerk designated solely for the purpose. One can hardly make a move without first of all consulting a circular which frequently refers to a future circular and to earlier consubstantial circulars.

Mr Burr revealed that Newport had started preparing for home defence as far back as 1936 when the medical officer of health organised a survey of buildings to identify those suitable for use as first-aid posts, decontamination centres and emergency hospital accommodation. However, according to Burr, there were other areas of concern. Officials had drawn up a list of vehicles that in an emergency could be used as ambulances and mobile first-aid units, but the traffic commissioners were dragging their feet over approving the scheme. The fleet of vehicles, many of which had been volunteered by private owners, were ruled out of action.

Pembroke Inferno

The Luftwaffe levelled Swansea to the ground, brought death and destruction to Cardiff, targeted Newport and other parts of Wales, but it was the West Wales port of Pembroke Dock that provided the enemy with probably its biggest Welsh scalp during the war.

A lone Nazi raider dived out of the sky at 3.15 p.m. on Monday 19 August 1940. A number of bombs were dropped on the government-owned oil tanks at Pennar on the east side of the town. One hit a storage tank, which burst into flames and sparked one of the biggest fires that Wales has ever seen. Men of the Auxiliary Fire Service from most parts of Wales and from Birmingham and Bristol descended to fight the inferno.

Five firefighters from Cardiff were killed. The story of their deaths was told by Home Office official Tom Breaks. He told the inquest how the men were 20 feet in front of him at work with a fire jet. 'Suddenly, there was a large burst of flame which seemed to envelop them,' he said. 'The last I saw of them was when they were retreating from the huge tongues of flame which shot out from everywhere.'

The Cardiff firemen who died were Clifford Mills (aged thirty) of Brunswick Street, Frederick Davies (thirty-one) of Llanbradach Street, Ivor Kilby (twenty-nine) of Gelligaer Street, Trevor Morgan (thirty-one) of May Street and John Thomas of Elaine Street. The city and Wales mourned these brave men. A memorial service was held at St Patrick's Church, Pennar.

More than 260 firefighters were injured at Pembroke Dock and the brave crews were machine-gunned by German raiders who returned to the area over a number of days. Forty men from Bristol had a miraculous escape when a bomb hit the Temperance Hall where they were resting. In total more than 600 men tackled the oil fires, which were not brought under control for three weeks. Eight tanks, each containing 12,000 tons of oil, were totally destroyed. Another eight tanks were saved. Smoke billowed thousands of feet into the air and the flames could be seen from the English side of the Bristol Channel.

Residents were evacuated from their homes in Military Road, Pennar, but the properties, which were threatened by the creeping flames, were saved by local firemen, led by Arthur Morris, who did not go to bed once during the three weeks. Firemen worked up to 19 hours a day before being stood down for a rest. A shortage of water, especially at low tide, added to the firefighters' problems. A trainload of foam arrived in the town but the substance was useless in containing the fire. Some of the oil tanks were deliberately blown up by the firefighters in a bid to stop the flames spreading, but this action met with little success.

Oil fire at Pembroke Dock.

There were many acts of bravery and George Medals were awarded to a number of firemen, including the regional fire chief and leader of Milford Haven fire brigade, Arthur Acornley. George Medals were also awarded to Fire Sergeant Daniel James Collins, Sub-Officer William Brown and Leading Fireman Norman Groom, all of Cardiff. Eight Bristol firemen and one from Birmingham were also decorated with George Medals. Mr A.R.B. Hart of Newport was made a Member of the Order of the British Empire.

Pembroke Dock's war nightmare was not over. On 21 May 1941 thirty-three people were killed and twenty-one seriously injured in a 3-hour raid which started at midnight. Five waves of bombers targeted the town using the pattern perfected over Swansea – incendiaries followed by heavy explosives, followed by incendiaries, followed by heavy explosives.

Many of the bombs landed in the mud near Front Street but others destroyed eighteen houses, several pubs and shops, and damaged some public buildings. Houses were demolished in Gwyther Street, Melville Street, Lawas Street and Market Street. The Prince Albert, Crichton and Three Crowns pubs and the Pier Hotel were all destroyed.

It was in the vicinity of the Pier Hotel, a few hundred yards from the Pembroke Dock–Neyland ferry terminal, that most died. A number of people sheltering in the basement of the hotel were killed when a high explosive struck the building – shades of what happened at the Hollyman Bakery in Grangetown, Cardiff, in January 1941 (see pp. 9–10). The licencee, Mr W. Morris, and his eighteen-year-old daughter Eileen were among the victims. Eileen's brother Derek was seriously injured.

The licencee of the Three Crowns, Alfred Bowen, and his wife were rescued alive from the ruins of their pub 14 hours after it had been destroyed by a bomb. Historian Harry Reynolds and his wife died when their house near the Three Crowns collapsed on them.

There was one outstanding act of foolhardy bravery by two young policemen, not named in contemporary accounts. They carried a delayed-action bomb from the garden of a house and tossed it into the sea from the pier. It exploded minutes later. One of the policemen had only just rescued his own wife and child from their home after it had been hit by a bomb.

The Germans made another unwelcome visit to Pembroke Dock on 11 June 1941. Property was damaged in New Street, Gwyther Street, Commercial Row, Market Street, Bush Street, Queen Street and Military Street. An airman died after protecting his wife from a bomb blast. She was only slightly hurt.

Pembrokeshire had a total of 243 air-raid alerts in the first four years of the war, but many of these were to warn of enemy aircraft flying over the county on the way to the Midlands and the North. A total of fifty-six people were killed by raids, most of them in Pembroke Dock

The rest of the county of Pembrokeshire suffered only scattered and usually light raids by lone bombers. Horses, cows and sheep were killed by bombs landing on farmland while there were occasional hits on isolated villages and on the foreshore. On 15 April 1941 thirteen airmen were killed when Carew Airfield was raided. Four women, all members of the same family, died when a bomb hit Kensington House, Hazelbeach, near Neyland on 11 June 1941, the night that Pembroke Dock was targeted. They were eighty-year-old Margaret Evans, her two daughters and seventeen-year-old granddaughter. The husband of one of the women and his son had just left the house and were treated only for shock. A group of people had a narrow escape when an unexploded bomb landed near them in a road at Bufferland.

There were apparently other German visitors to Pembrokeshire during the war. In later years a guide at St David's Cathedral was told by a German tourist that he served aboard a Nazi U-boat during the war and was one of the men who rowed ashore to collect fresh water supplies along the Pembrokeshire coast.

Firemen paying tribute to their Cardiff colleagues who died fighting the oil fire at Pembroke Dock.

Tenby Targeted

Tenby was right under the flight path of enemy bombers heading for Merseyside but it was not until 21 October 1941 that the West Wales resort was attacked. A lone raider dropped four bombs on the town, killing 76-year-old Mrs Hadyn Thomas. A bomb scored a direct hit on her house, St Roman's in Queen's Parade. Fifteen people were injured. A second bomb made a big crater at the back of houses in Church Park. A third fell on what was once a putting green near The Rectory and a fourth slammed into the top of Jubilee Walk, leading down to South Beach.

Bedsteads were straddled on roofs of houses in Harriet Street and Church Park, and items of furniture were thrown into streets some distance from the blast. Rhos Cottage, in Church Park, the home of blacksmith George Morris and his wife, was cut in half, and the couple were trapped in their bed with the roof hanging perilously over them. They were rescued by Civil Defence workers and treated in hospital. A retired bank manager, A.J. Newton, and his wife escaped serious injury when the roof of their home in Queen's Parade was ripped off by a bomb blast.

The town's deputy head warden, Captain A.C. Clanchy, was away on his first holiday since the war started when a bomb wrecked his home in Queen's Parade. The only occupant of the house, a Miss A. de Burg, escaped serious injury. Some coastguard cottages were destroyed and all the houses in Queen's Parade were damaged. Fourteen-month-old Janice Reid had a miraculous escape when heavy masonry fell on her cot at the Church Park home of her parents, Mr and Mrs Doug Reid.

When the mayor, Councillor Sydney Hughes, toured the town where he had worked through the night as a warden, he said he was proud to see Union flags flying from damaged houses – a symbol of the spirit of Tenby.

The Newton family escaped injury when a bomb blast ripped off the roof of their home in Queen's Parade in October 1941. *(Tenby Museum)*

Barry Spared

During the Second World War I was a schoolboy in my home town of Barry, which escaped very lightly considering the importance of the docks, which my family helped to build in the nineteenth century. Only six people were killed in just two fatal raids on the town.

The first fatal raid on Barry was on 30 April 1941 when Brenda Baxter (aged thirty-three), and her husband Tom (twenty-nine) of Cambridge Street, Ethel Dare (forty-two) and William Hopkins (forty-three), both of Oxford Street, and Melville Gibbs (four) of Romilly Park Road were all killed.

In the same raid houses on the Witchell Estate were also hit. My cousin Jean Elston, who was ten at the time, escaped injury when a kerbstone landed on her bed at 3 Dyfan Road. It had smashed through the roof after a high-explosive bomb fell less than 100 yards away. The first the family knew about the kerbstone was Jean picking grit from her hair as they sat in the Anderson shelter in their back garden. Jean's older sister Maisie and toddler brother John also escaped injury as did their mother Cissie and grandmother Mrs Boffy. Cissie's husband George Elston, my mother's brother, was fire-watching when the bomb fell. He was in the army and fought in the Battle of Monte Cassino in Italy. He died of cancer in the early 1960s.

During the raid hundreds of incendiary bombs fell in Porthkerry Park and on Cadoxton Moors. Boatmen claimed that this was because they misled the German pilots by moving the marker buoy in the Bristol Channel a few hundred yards. The buoy was apparently one of the landmarks used to pinpoint targets.

The only other fatal raid on the town was on 25 June 1944 when railway fireman Aubrey Fairfax of Cambridge Street died at Barry Docks. He was a nightwatchman on a ship in the graving dock when a landmine was dropped there.

Three Barry people died during the raid on Cardiff on 2/3 January 1941. They were Constance Blake, who died at Gold Street, Selina Brannan (aged sixty-nine) and Beatrice Tangye (forty-five) of St Nicholas Road, Barry, who both died at Blackstone Street. Frank Wakeham (fifty-four) of Pontypridd Road, Barry, was a captain in the Home Guard and was injured while on duty at Buckingham Palace on 5 August 1944. He died from his wounds at Whitchurch Hospital, Cardiff, on 10 November 1946.

The fact that Barry escaped major bomb damage is all the more puzzling when you consider the town's location. It was 7 miles from Grangetown and Riverside, which were flattened in the raids, and 14 miles from St Athan, one of the biggest air bases in the world.

Bob Griffiths and his son John Owen by the Anderson shelter in the garden of a house in Phyllis Street, Barry Island. *(Brian Luxton Archives)*

Barry graving dock after a landmine was dropped there in July 1941. *(Brian Luxton Archives)*

There was a large Army Supply Reserve Depot at the Bendricks and hundreds of American troops were based at Cadoxton Moors. Legend has it that these included future world boxing champion Rocky Marciano. He is said to have fought his first bout at the Wenvoe Arms (later renamed The Admiral). He laid out a few opponents when a scrap started at stop-tap. I remember us kids running after the American army lorries as they carried goods salvaged from sunken ships to the council refuse depot at Gladstone Road. In answer to our pleas they threw us chocolate and chewing gum.

But my most vivid memory is of the hundreds of troops, queuing four abreast, carrying rifles and haversacks and wearing full combat gear. I sold the *Echo* to them as they boarded special trains at Cadoxton station on the first leg of their journey to various ports to join the D-Day forces who invaded Normandy on 6 June 1944. God only knows how many of these men were killed in the following weeks.

Another memory from the war years is of a dogfight in the skies over Barry as a British Spitfire shot down a German raider. The German pilot died when the plane crashed in the woods at Sully. I was among the scores of people who gathered on Kenilworth Hill to watch the air battle.

SPY IN FACTORY

Legend has it that Barry Docks escaped a major blitz because the Germans planned to use them as a main supply port if they invaded Britain. This makes sense: the second highest tidal range in the world has been recorded at Barry, behind only Fundy Bay in Nova Scotia.

If there was a plan to make Barry a key port in the event of an invasion, it was almost certainly put forward by Fritz Richter, who was manager of the Enamel Works on Barry Docks from 1932 until 1939. He sent a message to his secretary in 1939 to tell her that he had escaped Britain after boarding a German merchant ship in the Irish Sea. When I asked for information about him in a letter to the *Barry and District News* in 1968, I received a letter from Mr G. Deighton of Clive Place, Barry Island, who had been employed at the Enamel Works from 1932 until it closed in 1969. He said he remembered Fritz Richter. He recalled that Richter had left Barry in a hurry at the time of the Munich Crisis in 1938, but said he had returned to the factory after the Prime Minister Neville Chamberlain came back from Germany waving a piece of paper and declaring 'Peace in our time'. Richter again left in a hurry, this time for good, just before Chamberlain declared war on Germany on 3 September 1939.

Deighton learnt that Richter had been an artillery captain in the German army during the First World War and had been wounded in action. Richter was a prominent figure at remembrance services at the Barry cenotaph in the 1930s. He was apparently an expert in the enamelling trade and helped to build up a successful business in the town.

Caerphilly, Ebbw Vale and Beyond

Historian Glyndwr G. Jones gave a vivid account of Caerphilly at war in papers that he deposited at Cardiff Central Library's local studies department and Caerphilly Library. He told how the 2nd Battalion of the Monmouthshire Regiment, led by their own band, arrived in the town on Sunday morning, 3 September 1939, the day Prime Minister Neville Chamberlain declared war on Germany. The battalion probably had the first fatal casualty of the war because on that Sunday a dispatch rider was killed as he fell from his motorcycle.

During the first few weeks of the war the band gave open-air concerts, while the troops set up field kitchens and prepared to defend the town and its famous castle against any would-be invader. Glyndwr Jones recalled the way Cardiff was protected by a circle of barrage balloons, a defence against low-flying aircraft. He also had vivid memories of searchlights based in Caerphilly lighting up German planes for the ack-ack crews on the ground.

The first bombs to land in the locality were three light-explosive weapons which hit the Bedwas area around midnight on 12 July 1940. The first fell between 43 and 46 Church Street and damaged the Wesleyan Chapel. The second bomb fell on the road outside 24 East Avenue. The house's doors and windows were blown out and the slates ripped off the roof. Furniture and fittings were badly damaged and seven other houses in the street were hit by shrapnel. The male occupant of number 24, George Davies, was working nights at the British Benzol Plant at Trethomas. Fortunately, his wife and three children had taken shelter under the stairs of their home and escaped serious injury. The third bomb fell in a field near Pantglas Farm, Trethomas.

Hundreds of incendiary bombs rained on the Caerphilly area but there were no human fatalities as a result of the raids. Seven sheep were killed by a bomb that landed at Rudry on 27 July 1940. On 18 August the same year eight bombs were dropped between Penyrheol and Abertridwr and most made huge craters in fields. One bomb damaged the railway line between Abertridwr and Caerphilly, but this was repaired the same day. On 1 September another bomb fell near the home of Glyndwr Jones in Energlyn, Caerphilly. When he visited the site the next day he found a crater 42 yards wide. Sitting near the edge of it was elderly Gypsy Lee, smoking his pipe. He had slept through the raid in his crude hut, which was only yards from the crater.

Some of the 900 evacuees from Kent arriving at Caerphilly in June 1940. *(Gatehouse)*

EVACUEES WELCOMED

In June 1940 Caerphilly welcomed more than 900 evacuees, including 80 adults, who arrived by train from Folkestone in Kent. The youngest of the 830 children was Margaret Colhan, who was just 12 months old. In addition 80 boys and a number of teachers from the Rochester and Gillingham Technical School were also billeted in the town.

On 7 November 1941 an allied plane, piloted by a Canadian, crashed on the south-west side of Caerphilly Mountain, not far from the Travellers' Rest pub. The pilot was killed. The crash was dealt with by Caerphilly firemen, who also helped to fight the fires after the raids on Cardiff, Swansea, Newport and other parts of South Wales. Caerphilly Home Guard also assisted in the rescue work in Cardiff.

American troops arrived in Caerphilly and other parts of South Wales in June 1942. They occupied a camp near the Pontygwindy Inn at Caerphilly, originally built by Glamorgan County Council to accommodate hundreds of evacuees from Cardiff, if the need arose. The Americans left Caerphilly to join the invasion forces in France in July 1944.

An Indian regiment with pack mules and a Gurkha regiment were billeted at Ruperra Castle for some time during the 1940s.

HAYRICK BEACON

The rural areas of Wales did not escape the blitz. Mr E. Verley, who in the late 1940s was secretary of the National Farmers' Union in Wales, recalled one of the twenty-three raids on Llantwit Major. The choice of target was not surprising as the historic town was on the edge of St Athan, one of the biggest RAF bases in the world. Verley had just finished a meal at a farmhouse when he was called outside to see a hayrick on fire in the distance. A German plane was caught in beams of one of the five searchlights sweeping the sky. Suddenly bombs started falling as the raiders used the burning hayrick as a beacon.

The women in the farmhouse were lying terrified on the floor as every window in the building was broken by the bomb blasts. In the town an historic chantry house was damaged and the stained-glass windows of the neighbouring church were smashed.

In another part of the vale the Adams family counted twelve near-miss bombs falling before the unlucky thirteenth scored a direct hit on the house where a couple and their five children were sleeping. Six of the family managed to get out but the seventh, a girl named Prudence, was trapped under the debris, only her head being visible. It took 45 minutes to free her, virtually unhurt.

The experience of the Vale of Glamorgan, which had its share of incendiaries and high explosives, was typical of the rural parts of Wales, according to the *Western Mail and Echo*'s booklet from the late 1940s, *Bombers Over Wales*. Among the areas targeted were St Athan, The Leys, Monknash, Rogiet, Wenvoe and Dinas Powys. Further west bombs fell on Cimla, Baglan, Skewen, Brynamman, Gorseinon and St Ishmaels. Every county in Wales was bombed at some point in the war.

Surprisingly, however, Ebbw Vale almost escaped attack during the Second World War, despite the importance of the steelworks. Local historian Gerry Jones recorded that one German reconnaissance plane took photographs of the works from a great height in December 1940. Copies of the photographs were found in official German records after the war. There was also a photograph in the official guide to Wales which was issued to Luftwaffe pilots. But the steelworks, where special precautions were taken to black out the furnaces at night, were not hit once. A great deal of money was invested in an anti-glare system to black out the furnaces and coke ovens. However, there may be a sinister reason why the Ebbw Vale steelworks and the one at Cardiff were spared. Had the Germans invaded Britain they would have wanted to produce steel for their own purposes. The works at Ebbw Vale did pay a high price for the war. More than a third of the 6,000-strong workforce was called up to serve in the armed forces and of those 33 were killed in action. Women were employed to fill the vacancies left by the servicemen.

The only attack on Ebbw Vale took place in September 1940, when a stick of bombs was dropped along the hilltop from Briery Hill to Sirhowy. There were no

A view of Ebbw Vale steelworks which was included in a book of Welsh targets issued to German pilots.

casualties but one bungalow near Capel Waunpound was damaged. Gerry Jones reported that thousands of sightseers went to the scene the day after the raid. The story of the Ebbw Vale Home Guard and its remarkable leader is told on p. 129.

PART TWO

The Welsh at War

HOME FROM HELL

There were cheers at football and rugby grounds throughout Wales when the news was flashed from Singapore on 11 September 1945 that 211 officers and men of the 77th Heavy Ack-Ack Regiment Royal Artillery had been liberated from Japanese prisoner-of-war camps. The regiment included the Sportsmen's Battalion, whose members' names were more likely to be found on team lists than a prison working schedule.

The 77th Heavy Ack-Ack was raised and trained in the Cardiff area. Legend has it that recruiting officers told the sportsmen who joined that they would spend the war entertaining troops and civilians on pitches across the country. This was true for the first months of the war, but their experience was to change as hostilities continued.

The regiment was based at Maerdy Farm in Rumney, where the men were taught to load and fire heavy ack-ack guns. Some of them were later based at Sloper Road, near Ninian Park football ground. They first fired their guns in anger at the German planes that bombed Cardiff, particularly in the vicious blitz on 2 and 3 January 1941. But on Saturdays in the relevant season the men were given leave to play soccer, rugby, cricket or hockey.

There were five members of the Cardiff City football team in the 77th: Ernie Curtis, who had played in the 1927 FA Cup-winning team, Billy James, Bobby Tobin, Billy Baker and goalkeeper Jackie Pritchard. James won a wartime cap against England in the early 1940s and the others volunteered as stewards so that they could get leave to see the match. In January 1941 Cardiff were due to play Swansea City at the Vetch Field on the Saturday after the town was bombed, but the match had to be cancelled because there were two unexploded bombs at the ground. In April 1941 Pritchard, James, Tobin and Baker all played for Cardiff City at Ninian Park against Tottenham Hotspur in front of a 20,000-strong crowd, many of whom were in military uniform. Billy James scored one of Cardiff's goals in the 2–2 draw.

The battalion's rugby players included Les Spence, Fred Street and Wilf Wooller, who was later captain of Glamorgan cricket team and was also on the books of Barry Town football club. The rugby players' series of matches at the Arms Park was interrupted when a landmine destroyed part of the ground in January 1941.

In February 1942 the 77th was sent to Java and its arrival almost coincided with the capitulation of the Dutch army there. Six weeks later the regiment, and its famous sportsmen, were prisoners of war.

More than 300 men of the 77th died at the hands of their Japanese captors. Others carried the scars of their treatment for decades. *South Wales Echo* war correspondent Victor Lewis sent this dispatch to Cardiff in time for the first edition on 12 September 1945.

Waiting patiently and cheerfully in the notorious Changi POW Camp are 200 men and 11 officers, who in a matter of days will be sailing for Britain –

300 Welsh A.A. Men Died In Captivity

Java Survivors Now Await Liberation

Top: Grim news in the *Western Mail*, September 1945.

Above: Welshmen were among these prisoners of war in Japan.

Right: Cardiff City players Bobby Tobin and Billy James. *(Cardiff City Library)*

Cardiff and home. They will bring with them scores of tales of horror, heroism and tragedy – and a saga of undying courage and unfailing morale in the face of a greater battle against disease, ill-treatment and starvation than was probably fought by any other units which fell into Japanese hands.

They are some of the survivors of the 77th. Their epic story is written on six sheets of rice paper. It is a story which will thrill and horrify South Wales, for it runs the whole gamut of war's worst experiences. Today I have talked with scores of the men who lived through three years of hell in Java, Singapore and Siam. They included Cardiff City players Ernie Curtis, Billy James, Bobby Tobin and Jackie Pritchard.

Sadly this report was not entirely true, as it was later learnt that 35-year-old Lance Sergeant Jackie Pritchard, whose parents Thomas and Mary lived at St Fagans, and whose wife Edith Patty Pritchard lived in Fairwater, Cardiff, had died on 23 July 1943, apparently when a Japanese ship carrying prisoners was sunk. His full name, William John Pritchard, is on the memorial at Kanchanaburi War Cemetery in Thailand. Other members of the 77th are either buried in the cemetery or remembered on the memorial.

Many of the 13,000 Allied prisoners who died building the infamous Burma–Siam railway are also buried in the cemetery. An estimated 80,000 to 100,000 civilians also died in the course of the project, chiefly forced labour brought from Malaya and the Dutch East Indies, or conscripted in Siam (Thailand) and Burma (Myanmar).

Bluebird Billy Baker was among the survivors and he and Bobby Tobin played for Cardiff after the war. Billy James survived but never played first-class football again. I was privileged to meet him shortly before he died at Rookwood Hospital, Cardiff, in the 1960s.

The *Echo* reporter's 1945 account continued.

I looked for an old friend, Bombardier Albert Love, who took part in the Empire Games at Ottawa in 1930. I learnt from the CO Lt Col H.R. Humphries that he had died from the dreaded beri-beri in Java. Taking their first taste of freedom, I found Lt John Rutter, son of Edgar J. Rutter, of Cardiff; Major Gerald Gaskell, of Hancocks Breweries; Capt Sir William J.C. Thomas, and Capt H.M. Lloyd, a well-known Bridgend lawyer. Just outside the camp, wallowing in the luxury of a sea bathe, I found Lt Wilfred Wooller, famous Welsh rugby international.

I heard from Col Humphries that safe in Java were Capt Geoffrey Ash and Lt Alan Reardon-Smith, son of Welsh ship owner Sir William Reardon-Smith, some of whose ships are today in Singapore Roads bringing in supplies. Also safe in Java are former Cardiff High School masters Lt G. Davies and Lt W. Salmon.

Home from hell, Sappers Dunn and Morgan, both of Cardiff.

The story also confirmed that Battalion Sergeant Major Les Spence, the Cardiff rugby forward, was in Java, where the 77th had been captured in 1942 before most of them were transferred to other prison camps in Thailand and Burma.

Shortly before the regiment had been forced to surrender three years earlier, Lieutenant-Colonel H.R. Humphries had about 1,000 men under his command. The casualty figures provided to the reporter by Humphries gave some idea of the living hell endured by the men, who were mostly recruited in Cardiff and surrounding areas. The reporter wrote:

Some were beaten to death in Siam; others died of starvation, despite the heroic efforts of Col Humphries, who frequently defied the Japanese and risked death to get adequate food for them. Still more died of beri-beri, cholera and malaria, against which it was almost impossible to fight in the jungles of Siam when the Japanese refused medical supplies.

The 77th fought its first battle against the Japanese on 24 February 1942 and the men acquitted themselves well against overwhelming odds. On 29 March, fourteen weeks after they had played their last rugby and soccer games in Cardiff, the 77th were unwilling guests of the Japanese at Glodok gaol.

Sergeant T.O. Jones of Gilfach Goch with his wife and child and his friend Private Hurley of Senghnydd.

Lance-Corporal Hillman and F. Presswood, both of Treorchy, greeted by family and friends.

Glodok was a filthy hole and Colonel Humphries described the food as appalling – nothing but rice, served by native convicts who brought it in coal bags. After a year in this camp the prisoners were split up and sent to gaols throughout the Far East.

War correspondent Victor Lewis sent an account of the prison camps back to the *Echo* in Cardiff on 15 September 1945. This is the tale as related to Lewis:

The jungle hell of the 77th started in May 1943. Lt Col H.R. Humphries, their commanding officer, was selected to take charge of the tragic force, destined to work and starve and die in Siam on the railway project of terrible memory. Col Humphries went into the jungle at the head of 3,500 men (300 from the 77th). He came back with only 886 men. The rest had died of starvation or disease or had been beaten to death.

In Changi prisoner-of-war camp [where the survivors were waiting to be returned to Britain], men closed their eyes and shuddered at the memory of those months. . . . Long before he was put to work on the railway, each man was utterly tired and half-starved. But the Japanese forced the men to dig embankments, blast obstructions and even to build bridges. These were the men who were clerks and lawyers, businessmen and men in the professions [in South Wales]. They knew nothing of the art of railway building, but every time they made a mistake they were beaten.

All through their captivity, wherever they were, they held weekly meetings of the Welsh Society. These men, many of whom were only technically alive, held their own eisteddfodau. Colonel Humphries took up the story:

Patients were brought to the camp hospital in trucks on the nightmare railway they had slaved to build. They came in like living skeletons in a ghastly crawling line. But their spirit was incredible. In the filthy night, from this filthy shack which was their haven, the songs of Wales would ring out until the whole jungle echoed to 'Land of My Fathers' or 'Cwm Rhondda'.

The men of the 77th made a roll of honour, carved from jungle timber. The prison church in which it hung was demolished but the roll was later found and restored. A relic of the jungle chapel now hangs in Tabernacle Chapel, The Hayes, Cardiff. Colonel Humphries had another relic, kept in a tin box, a wooden crest, bearing the colours of the Royal Artillery surmounted by a leek and bearing the motto 'Betoel!' – the Malaysian word for 'The Goods'. Reporter Jenkins finished his dispatch with his own personal view: 'Never was there a more apt motto. By their courage, their bearing, their fortitude, the 77th have earned the right to regard themselves eternally as The Goods.'

The Mossford family in Cardiff had every reason to believe that Major Clive Mossford had died while a prisoner of war in Japan. His wife Madge received a letter from the War Office expressing regret at her husband's death. And there was confirmation in a cable sent from Singapore by Welsh rugby international and Glamorgan cricket captain Wilf Wooller, who had served in the 77th Heavy Ack-Ack with Major Mossford and had also spent some time in a prisoner-of-war camp with him. Mossford was believed to have been lost on a Japanese ship that was sunk in 1943 en route to an island prison camp.

But Major Mossford was very much alive and came back to Cardiff some weeks after VJ Day in 1945. He returned to the family's monumental sculpture business and continued working until his death in 1974.

Major Mossford had been actively connected with the Territorial Army and went on active service as soon as the war broke out. His only son Clive was born in 1940 and was two when his father went to Java with the 77th in February 1942. When I met Clive Mossford in 1995 his mother was living in Penarth. He was the managing director of Lion Laboratories at Barry, the company that pioneered the Breathalyser. He told me, 'I was only five when my father was reported dead, but I remember being at Cardiff General Station when he came home from the war. My family certainly believed that he had died while a prisoner, but my father rarely spoke of his ordeal at the hands of the Japanese.'

The Mossford family was just one of many in Britain to be wrongly told that a loved one had been killed in action. Olive, the wife of John Murray of the Parade, Barry, had been mourning her husband for five months before she learnt, in April 1941, that he

Bombardier M. Simons of Cardiff linking arms with his wife and mother.

was a prisoner of war in Germany. Murray was an engineer on the SS *Port Wellington*, which was reported sunk on a voyage from Australia to England in the autumn of 1940. He was a former captain of the Barry water polo team and of Brynhill Golf Club. He married Olive Ashton a few weeks before his ship sailed to Australia.

Survivors of the 77th Heavy Ack-Ack landed in Liverpool aboard the New Zealand liner *Monowai* and travelled on to Cardiff by train. One in six of the ex-prisoners had lost track of their loved ones and didn't know whether they or their homes had been victims of the blitz. The *South Wales Echo* reported that the vast majority of the 650 service personnel and 199 civilians aboard the liner were suffering from malnutrition.

Those on board included 91 officers and 400 other ranks from the army; 1 officer and 22 Royal Navy ratings; 5 officers and 36 other ranks from the RAF; and 5 Merchant Navy officers. The civilians comprised 163 men, 29 women and 7 children. The *Monowai* was the first of thirty-six ships due at Liverpool with ex-prisoners of war on board.

When they arrived back in South Wales the survivors were given a civic reception at City Hall. Among them was Ted Weston of Barry, a brother-in-law of my mother's sister, Min Weston. He died shortly after the fiftieth anniversary of VJ Day. On his return Wilf Wooller was surprised to learn that news of his capture in Java in 1942 had been received in South Wales via a radio message from Japan which was picked up in New Zealand.

LETTERS TO FAMILIES

In 1945 families waited anxiously for news from their loved ones, especially those who had been in prisoner-of-war camps in the Far East. The *Echo* reported on some of the letters received in South Wales.

Aircraftsman Bernard Cox, whose late father had been a doctor in Taffs Well, was one of only 250 prisoners who survived the notorious Ambon prisoner-of-war camp where at least 750 of his colleagues died. In his first letter home to his mother in September 1945, the 25-year-old wrote, 'The lads are all cheerful, although we are not in the best of health due to lack of food and the rough treatment.' He said that during captivity he was taken back to Java to hospital for seven months. It took four days to reach Ambon, but seventy-eight days to return. Of 600 men on the ship, 300 died. Cox had sailed for the Far East on his twenty-first birthday. His father died a few months before Bernard was taken prisoner.

In a letter to his parents in Tyn-y-Parc Road, Whitchurch, ex-prisoner Aircraftsman Ronald Read wrote, 'I feel quite proud with a pair of nice white socks on and boots – a thing we haven't seen for about three years.'

Aircraftsman Second Class R.C.C. James of Hanover Street, Canton, Cardiff, wrote to tell his wife he was working in the office of a large women's camp while waiting to be shipped home.

There were tears at the home of the Weaver family in Howell Street, Cilfynydd, when a letter arrived from ex-prisoner Private David Weaver to say he was safe in a camp at Melbourne, Australia. The message was addressed to his mother who had died some months earlier.

Major J.M. Lloyd of the Royal Artillery wrote to his wife at the Retreat in Penylan, Cardiff, to say he was waiting for the RAF to fly him home from India. Major Lloyd had been taken prisoner in Singapore in 1942. His wife was the daughter of the late Sir Charles Bird, a former lord mayor of Cardiff. Major Lloyd worked for John Bland, timber importers, before joining the army in 1940.

Also waiting for a flight home from India was Lieutenant Charles Merlin Williams who sent a cable to his wife Betty in Tewkesbury Place, Cardiff, to say he was safe. Since his capture at the fall of Singapore in 1942, his wife had received only four postcards from him.

Lance-Corporal Kenneth Mugford of the Royal Engineers cabled his wife in Llandaff to say he was safe in Allied hands. The joy was shared by his parents who lived in Paget Street, Grangetown, a street that was bombed in January 1941.

A PRICE ON HIS HEAD

A Barry man whom I interviewed for the *Barry Herald* in the 1950s, after playing a game of bowls with him at the town's Central Park, played a major role in the battle against the Japanese in Burma. Brigadier Arthur Felix-Williams had a £10,000 price put on his head by the Japanese while winning a unique place in military history. His James Bond-style role began in 1942 when the Old Barrian was ordered by Field Marshal Earl Wavell, then Commander-in-Chief in India, to raise the world's first massive guerrilla army. The job of the volunteer force was to spy on the enemy, to harry, destroy and kill, and above all to hold the India–Burma frontier for six months.

Felix-Williams had a brigade force of 140 men and women and a budget of £1 million, including £150,000 in gold and £100,000 in silver. The brigadier and his henchmen raised an army of 18,000 civilians, a phantom horde known as the V-Force. It held the vital frontier for more than two years. The money was used to pay tribal chieftains and to help establish a long chain of arms and food dumps to be used when the Allies began their big advance.

Brigadier Arthur Felix-Williams.

When I met the brigadier at Barry he told me that some of the guns for the V-Force were bought in the bazaars of Calcutta. Others, including blunderbusses and long muzzle-loading rifles, had been seized from tribesmen on India's north-west frontier. The Barry man's huge force of tea planters and tribesmen was in action long before Orde Wingate and his celebrated Chindits began their long-range raids in Burma.

One of the people enlisted by Felix-Williams was Ursula Bowers, a 28-year-old English woman who went to the Naga hills of Assam in 1939 to study anthropology. The so-called 'Queen of the Nagas' organised the men of the tribe as part of the V-Force.

Felix-Williams, whose father was a chairman of the former Barry Urban Council, had served with the army in India for twenty years before the outbreak of the Second World War and clashed with tribal warriors on the north-west frontier in the 1920s.

When he played bowls with me at Barry in the 1950s he was on leave from Kenya, where he had elected to serve to fight the Mau Mau. He went to live with his children, Maureen and John, in Chicago in the early 1960s and died there in 1965 at the age of 69.

Another Barry man also played a key role in the Burma Campaign. Captain Leonard Davies, whose story was told in the 'Stroller' column of the *South Wales Echo* in May 1945, was affectionately known as 'The Professor' in the legendary Chindits force. The Old Barrian was in the Army Education Corps and was education officer at the Chindits Headquarters in India. He was responsible for giving or arranging 2,500 lectures to members of the Chindits army on current affairs, politics and economics. He organised debates, 'brains trusts', handicraft classes and musical evenings. Captain Davies, the son of Mr and Mrs Bert Davies of St Nicholas Road, Barry, was a graduate of the University of Wales in Cardiff. While there, he wrote a thesis on the history and development of Barry Docks and the former Barry Railway Company.

A GAP IN THE BAMBOO CURTAIN

World table-tennis supremo H. Roy Evans brought off a major diplomatic coup in the 1960s when he was invited to have tea with Chairman Mao, leader of China. As reported exclusively by my *South Wales Echo* colleague Alec McKinty, it was the first sporting chink in the bamboo curtain – Roy, who lived in Cyncoed, Cardiff, paved the way for China to join the International Table-Tennis Federation, of which he was president. This was also the first step on the long road to China's hosting the Olympic Games in 2008.

Twenty years before his visit to China, Roy was serving as a flight lieutenant with the Royal Air Force in Burma. On VJ Day he heard a voice he recognised singing 'The Road to Mandalay' at a victory concert. It was Corporal Ivor Humphreys, a noted singer from Pontypridd, who joined the RAF with Roy in the early days of the war. He was the star guest at the concert on Roy's station.

HOME TOWN GIRL

Close to VJ Day, former *Echo* rugby writer Reg Pelling wrote to the editor from Rangoon to tell him that he had seen a white woman for the first time in nearly four years – and she turned out to be from Reg's home town of Newport.

She was Mary Glassbrook, of Brynglas Road. (Her sister had been a beauty queen in the town in the mid-1930s.) Quartermaster Pelling wrote, 'Mary is one of the WVS who are doing grand work in Rangoon.' Reg, who had been a prisoner of the Japanese, met Mary at Mingaladon Airport when she escorted him and other ex-prisoners to a restroom and gave them tea, sandwiches, fruit, cream and cigarettes.

Reg was not the only *Western Mail and Echo* man to be a prisoner of war. Rex Reynolds, night editor of the *Western Mail*, was a prisoner in Japan. Dick Mills, who became chief sub-editor on the *Western Mail*, and Stan Williams, who worked in the library, were both held in German camps.

THE SURVIVORS

The sea claimed the lives of hundreds of seamen from South Wales during the Second World War and a list of the victims who died sailing out of Cardiff can be found in the Chapel of the Seaman's Mission at Cardiff Bay. But few people suffered more than Robert Tapscott and Roy Widdicombe, whose ill-fated voyage on the *Anglo-Saxon* started at Newport on 5 August 1940.

The vessel was sixteen days out of Newport on its way to Bahia Bianca and Buenos Aires (both in Argentina) when it was attacked by a German raider, believed to be the *Wesser*. The *Anglo-Saxon* was pounded by pom-pom shells and raked by machine-gun fire. Most of the crew were killed but Tapscott, who came from Cardiff, and Widdicombe, a Devon man who was married to Cynthia Pitman of Newport, were among seven men who survived by hurling themselves into an 18-foot jolly boat.

They were nearly 1,000 miles from the Canary Islands and more than 2,000 miles from the Bahamas. They had one tin of ship's biscuit, eleven tins of condensed milk, three tins of mutton and four gallons of water. The water lasted just fifteen days. Two of the men died of wounds, leaving the other five to live on half a biscuit a day, some scraps of mutton and one cup of water while it lasted. After twelve days their mouths were so dry they were unable to chew the hard biscuits.

On 23 September, some thirty-three days after they had left the stricken *Anglo-Saxon*, two of the five committed suicide by just slipping over the side of the boat. Tapscott and Widdicombe wept as they saw the men floating away, clasped in each other's arms. The food was gone. The water was gone. Tapscott, who was only nineteen, disciplined himself not to drink sea-water. He and Widdicombe poured it over themselves in an effort to dispel the agonies of thirst.

A few days later the third man, his name was Morgan and he came from Newport, said quietly: 'I'm going down the road for a drink.' He also stepped over the side and floated away. Widdicombe took out the log, which he had ceased keeping some time earlier, and wrote: 'Second cook gone mad; dies. Only two of us left.'

Stomach cramps plagued them. There had been no rain since the sinking of the *Anglo-Saxon*. Tapscott broke his vow and drank a little sea-water, but he was

The jolly boat from the *Anglo-Saxon*. *(O'Sullivan archives)*

violently sick and lay back weaker and more thirsty than before. They both decided to commit suicide and actually went over the side of the boat. But Widdicombe pulled himself out. 'I'm not, if you're not,' said Tapscott and somehow hauled himself back into the boat.

To ease their thirst the men decanted the raw alcohol from the compass into two empty condensed milk tins. It tore at their throats and burned their stomachs – but gradually they managed to grin. It helped them to forget the pain and the dangers and allowed them the luxury of hope.

They slept and on the following day rain lashed down into the sloping canvas they had prepared for it. They scraped at the canvas with their tins in their eagerness to gather the precious liquid. They ate seaweed and small crabs, which they found clinging to the weed. Then came a storm with tremendous lightning flashes. Waves lifted the skiff to their peaks and hurled it into their troughs. As the storm calmed a boat passed about half a mile away without spotting them.

Roy Widdicombe (left) and Robert Tapscott (in arms of a helper) at E Leuthera in the Bahamas. *(O'Sullivan archives)*

By this time both Widdicombe and Tapscott had each lost more than 6 stone in weight. They were unkempt, ragged skeletons of men with sunken eyes and erupted flesh. Then on 30 October 1940 – seventy days after the loss of the *Anglo-Saxon* – they landed at E Leuthera in the Bahamas. They were carried by local people to the area commissioner and admitted to hospital in Nassau where their visitors included the Duke and Duchess of Windsor. The Duke, who had abdicated for love of Mrs Simpson, was Governor of Bermuda.

Tapscott and Widdicombe were suffering from starvation, exposure and prolonged thirst. Their mental and nervous systems were badly deranged. They suffered insomnia and were frequently hysterical or depressed. Tapscott was near to death when he was admitted to hospital.

The men were sent back to Britain by different routes. Roy Widdicombe was on the liner *Siamese Prince*, which was torpedoed off the coast of Scotland on

3 February 1941. There were no survivors. Tapscott came back to Cardiff where he lived with his mother in Cowbridge Road East. He never recovered from his ordeal and was reluctant to talk about the nightmare when I met him in a Tiger Bay pub in the early 1960s. In September 1963 he died in a gas-filled sitting-room of a house in South Clive Street, Grangetown. The last survivor of the *Anglo-Saxon* had gone. His widow, whom I interviewed in Cardiff in 1995, believed that her husband's death was accidental. 'He never got over the ordeal of the sea, but he cherished life,' she said.

THE BATTLE OF NARVIK

In Ofotfjord, Narvik, Norway, on 10 April 1940 North Walian Captain Bernard Warburton-Lee of HMS *Hardy* led a flotilla of five destroyers in a surprise attack on German destroyers and merchant ships in a blinding snowstorm. The attack was successful, and was almost immediately followed by an engagement with five more German destroyers, during which Captain Warburton-Lee was mortally wounded by a shell that hit the *Hardy*'s bridge. He was the first person in the Second World War to be awarded the Victoria Cross, albeit posthumously. He is buried in Norway. Captain Warburton-Lee was born at Broad Oak, Redbrook, Flintshire (now Clwyd), in 1895.

Another Welshman was also decorated for bravery at Narvik. Warrant Officer Emrys Morgan, the son of a miner from Cardiff Road, Quaker's Yard, Merthyr, was awarded the Distinguished Service Medal for conspicious gallantry while serving on HMS *Aurora* during the raid.

Captain Bernard Warburton-Lee VC.

ATTACK ON ST NAZAIRE

One of the most famous and tragic actions by the British navy and the Commandos during the Second World War was the attack on the west French port of St Nazaire on 27 March 1942, two days before the thirty-fourth birthday of Lieutenant-Commander Stephen Halden Beattie.

Beattie, who was born at Leighton in Montgomeryshire, was one of five men to be awarded the Victoria Cross for their courage and daring at the German-controlled port. He was in command of HMS *Campbeltown*, an ancient American destroyer which, as ordered, he successfully deployed as a battering ram against the lock gates of the port. He then scuttled the ship, which was loaded with time-bombs that later exploded and destroyed the entrance to the key dry docks. The raid also involved eighteen little ships, mainly motor launches.

The destruction of the lock gates was intended to hinder the progress of the giant German battleship *Tirpitz*, which had showed no mercy to Allied shipping in the Atlantic. The dry dock at St Nazaire, which had been built in peacetime for the French liner *Normandie*, was one of only a handful in the world which was big enough to deal with the *Tirpitz*. When the lock gates were destroyed the battleship would have to return to Germany rather than St Nazaire for repairs, leaving it vulnerable to air and sea attacks. (The battleship was attacked by British midget submarines in October 1942 and September 1943. British carrier aircraft attacked her in April 1944 and she was eventually put out of action for good when the RAF hit her with a 12,000lb Tallboy bomb in September 1944.)

Of the 611 soldiers and sailors who took part in Operation Chariot at St Nazaire, 169 were killed and 216, including Beattie, were taken prisoner. Most of them were wounded. Beattie was rescued from the *Campbeltown* but the rescue vessel was sunk and the Welshman was one of only a few members of the *Campbeltown*'s crew to survive the action. One of those who died was Lieutenant Nigel Tibbits, who had been at the wheel when the destroyer rammed the lock gates. It was Tibbits who had devised the means by which the destroyer had been turned into a weapon of destruction.

The citation for Beattie's Victoria Cross described how, under intense fire directed on the bridge from a range of about 100 yards, and in the full blinding glare of many searchlights, he steamed *Campbeltown* into the lock gates as instructed, and beached and scuttled her in the correct position. Other decorations awarded to Beattie included the Croix de Guerre avec Palmes and Legion d'Honneur (France).

Others who won the Victoria Cross at St Nazaire were: Sergeant T.F. Durrant, Royal Engineers and No. 1 Commando (posthumous); Lieutenant-Colonel A.C. Newman, Essex Regiment and No. 2 Commando; Commander R.E.D. Ryder RN; and Able Seaman W.A. Savage, Royal Navy Volunteer Reserve (posthumous). Some 4 men were made members of the Distinguished Service Order, 17 were awarded Distinguished Service Crosses, 11 were given the Military Medal, 24 got the Distinguished Service Medal, 4 received the Conspicuous Service Medal and no fewer than 26 were Mentioned in Dispatches. Only 242 of the Chariot force returned immediately to British shores.

Stephen Beattie, an old boy of Abberley Hall, Rugby, joined the Royal Navy in 1925. Six years after he was freed from the prisoner-of-war camp he was promoted to the rank of captain. From 1952 to 1954 he was senior officer of an Australian frigate squadron and from 1956 to 1958 he was the senior naval officer in the Persian Gulf (his period in this post included the Suez Crisis in 1956). In the late 1950s he commanded HMS *Birmingham* and he retired from the navy in 1960.

From 1965 to 1969 he was naval adviser to the Ethiopian government. Married with four sons, he died on 24 April 1975 at Mullion, Cornwall, at the age of sixty-seven. There is a memorial on his grave at Ruan Minor churchyard in Cornwall.

SUPER SUBMARINER

Newport-born submariner John Tubby Linton was acclaimed as one of the greatest naval commanders of the Second World War. He was awarded the VC after being reported missing, but it was some weeks before his death was confirmed, his vessel having been sunk in the Tyrrhenian Sea with the loss of all hands.

He took command of the *Turbulent* in 1941 and by 1943 he and his crew had sunk thirty-one enemy ships. Linton's VC citation read:

> He sank one cruiser, one destroyer, one U-Boat, 28 supply ships, some 100,000 tons in all, and destroyed three trains by gunfire.
>
> In his last year he spent 254 days at sea, submerged for nearly half the time, and his ship was hunted 13 times and had 250 depth charges aimed at her. His many and brilliant successes were due to his constant activity and skill and the daring which never failed him when there was an enemy to be attacked.
>
> On one occasion he sighted a convoy of twin merchantmen and two destroyers in the mist and moonlight. He worked around ahead of the convoy and dived to attack it as it passed through the moon's rays. On bringing his sights to bear he found himself right ahead of a destroyer. He held his course till the destroyer was almost on top of him and when his sights came on the convoy he fired. His great courage and determination were rewarded. He sank one merchantman and one destroyer outright and set the other merchantman on fire so that she blew up.

The underwater hero was nicknamed 'Seven Ship Linton' after the *Turbulent* sank seven vessels in March 1943. Two months earlier he had become 'Linton the Train Wrecker'. The railway on Italy's Calabrian coast was being used by the Germans to transport enemy troops and supplies to the heel of Italy. The *Turbulent* surfaced and shelled the trains, causing chaos. But on what was, sadly, to be his last patrol as commander of the *Turbulent*, Tubby

Commander John Tubby Linton VC.

Linton and his crew died somewhere in the depth of the seas which they had ruled for so long.

In 1944 Commander Linton's fourteen-year-old son William, wearing Dartmouth Naval College uniform, received his father's Victoria Cross from King George VI at Buckingham Palace. Seven years later William was aboard the submarine *Affray* when she sank with the loss of all hands while on a training exercise in the English Channel.

TASKER'S LEADERSHIP

Fans and players know Mr Justice Tasker Watkins as the president of the Welsh Rugby Union. The legal profession and defendants remember him as a judge and QC. History records that this slightly built man from Nelson in Mid Glamorgan was one of the greatest heroes of the Second World War. He was awarded the Victoria Cross in November 1944 when he was a major in the Welch Regiment. The citation stated:

That while commanding a company of the Welch Regiment in north-west Europe (France) on August 16, 1944, the battalion was ordered to attack objectives near the railway at Balfour. Major Watkins' company had to cross open cornfields in which booby traps had been set. It was dark and the

company came under fire. The only officer left, Major Watkins placed himself at the head of his men and under short-range fire charged two enemy posts in succession, personally killing or wounding the occupants with his sten gun.

On reaching his objective he found an anti-tank gun manned by a German soldier. His sten gun jammed and he threw it in the German's face and shot him with his pistol before he had time to recover.

The company had only 30 men left and was counter-attacked by 50 enemy infantry. Major Watkins directed the fire of his men and led a bayonet charge which resulted in almost the complete destruction of the enemy.

At dusk orders were given for the battalion to withdraw. The orders were not received by Major Watkins' company, who found themselves alone and surrounded. Their numbers were

Major Tasker Watkins VC.

depleted and the light was failing. Major Watkins decided to rejoin his battalion by passing round the flank of the enemy position through which he had advanced, but while moving through the cornfields he was challenged by an enemy post at close range. After ordering his men to scatter, he charged the post with a bren gun and silenced it. He then led the remnants of his company back to battalion headquarters. His supreme gallantry and total disregard for his own safety saved the lives of his men and had a decisive influence on the course of the battle.

Major Watkins is the son of Mr and Mrs Bertram Watkins, who lived in Shingring Road, Nelson. They had another son and three daughters in various branches of the service during the war. An old boy of Pontypridd Grammar School, Tasker Watkins was an all-round sportsman, competing at rugby, cricket and cross-country running.

COAL AND COURAGE

Edward Chapman was one of the last men to be awarded the Victoria Cross during the Second World War. The former Welsh miner from Pontllanfraith joined the Monmouthshire Regiment in 1940 and was posted to the 2nd Battalion. He first saw action in June 1944 when his battalion landed in Normandy as part of the 160th Brigade in the 53rd Welsh Division. He was a corporal commanding a section throughout the fighting on the beachhead and was wounded in the breakout at Falaise in August 1944.

Edward Chapman VC.

When he came out of hospital five weeks later he was posted to the 3rd Battalion and saw action with it in the Low Countries in the autumn of 1944, and in the crossing of the Rhine and the advance into Germany in 1945. He won his Victoria Cross during the advance on Osnabrück after the crossing of the Dortmund–Ems Canal.

On 2 April 1945 the 3rd Battalion began what became repeated and costly attacks on the thickly wooded ridge of the Teutoberger Wald. This symbolically important forest was held by a fanatically dedicated force of German officer cadets and their instructors from the Officer School in Hanover, who were making a last stand. Chapman was leading his company's advance along a narrow track through the woods when a machine-gun opened fire at short range inflicting heavy casualties and causing considerable confusion. Chapman seized his company's bren gun and advanced alone. Firing from the hip he mowed down many of the opposition from point-blank range and forced the others to retire in disorder. At this point Chapman's company was also ordered to retire. But the order did not reach Chapman and his section was left isolated in its advanced position.

The Germans moved in and delivered a number of bayonet charges under cover of intense machine-gun fire. Chapman rose again with his bren gun to meet the assaults and on each occasion halted the attackers with his accurate fire. He was soon running out of ammunition, so he shouted to the survivors of his section for more bandoliers. He dropped into a fold in the ground, rolled on his back and covered those bringing up the ammunition by firing the bren gun over his shoulder. The Germans made every effort to eliminate him with grenades but with his magazine reloaded he again closed in and drove them off. During his men's withdrawal Chapman's company commander was severely wounded and was lying in the open, a short distance from Chapman's position. Still under heavy fire, Chapman reached the wounded officer and carried him back to comparative safety, but as he did so the officer was hit again; the round wounded Chapman in the thigh too. When he reached cover he found that the company commander was dead. Chapman refused to be evacuated until the position was finally secured.

Chapman left the army after the war but rejoined the 2nd Mons in 1948. Five years later he was awarded the British Empire Medal for outstanding service to the Territorial Army. He retired from the TA in 1957 with rank of company sergeant major.

When I met Ted Chapman at his home in Newport in the early 1990s he was a successful breeder of Welsh Mountain ponies and often attended Royal Welsh shows. He was also a keen fly-fishing enthusiast. In the mid-1980s he had accepted my invitation to unveil a headstone in St Mary's Churchyard, Whitchurch, Cardiff. It marks the grave of Charles Burley Ward, the last man to receive the Victoria Cross from Queen Victoria herself. Ward, who was given the honour for bravery in the South African War, died in 1922, but his grave remained unmarked until, with the valuable help of David Clarke and the Family History Society of which he was secretary, the grave was located and a suitable headstone placed there in the presence of Burley Ward's son and daughters.

Ted Chapman died early in 2002 at the age of eighty-two.

DUNKIRK, ARNHEM AND BEYOND – MORE VCS WITH WELSH CONNECTIONS

The day after Edward Chapman won the VC another Welshman, 25-year-old Captain Ian Oswald Liddell, earned the Victoria Cross for his action in securing a bridge over the River Ems at Lingen. The following details are taken from the *London Gazette* of 5 June 1945.

In Germany on April 3rd, 1945, Captain Ian Liddell was commanding a company of the Coldstream Guards ordered to capture intact a bridge over the river Ems, near Lingen. The bridge was heavily defended and prepared for demolition. Captain Liddell ran forward alone to neutralise the 500lb charges. Unprotected, and all the time under intense fire, he crossed and re-crossed the whole length of the bridge, disconnecting the charges at both ends and underneath it.

The bridge was captured intact, and the way cleared for the advance over the river. Captain Liddell's outstanding gallantry and superb example of courage will never be forgotten by those who saw it. This very brave officer died later in 1945 of wounds received in action.

Ian Liddell was the son of Percy William Oswald and Gwendoline Ray Liddell of Shirenewton, Monmouthshire. His wife, Patricia Mary Liddell, lived in Great Canfield, Essex.

Welsh Guardsman Lieutenant Christopher Furness was awarded the Victoria Cross for outstanding bravery during the retreat from Dunkirk in 1940. He was the son of Marmaduke Furness, who was 1st Viscount Furness, and of the Viscountess Furness (née Hogg), of Westminster, London. The citation in the *London Gazette* of 5 February 1946 gave the following details.

The Hon Christopher Furness was in command of the Carrier Platoon, Welsh Guards, from May 17th–24th, 1940, at Arras, in France. His extremely high degree of leadership and dash imbued his command with a magnificent offensive spirit during their constant patrols and many local actions throughout this period. On May 22nd, 1940, he was wounded, but refused to be evacuated. The enemy had encircled the town on three sides, and Lt Furness's platoon, together with a small force of light tanks, were ordered to cover the withdrawal of over 40 transport vehicles to Douai. Heavy small arms and anti-tank gunfire blocked the column. Lt Furness, realising the seriousness of the situation, with three carriers and the light tanks attacked at close quarters the strongly entrenched enemy, inflicting heavy losses. His carriers were hit, most of their crews killed or wounded, and the tanks were put out of action. When his own carrier was disabled and the driver and gunner killed, Lt Furness, despite his wounds, engaged the enemy in hand to hand combat until he was killed.

His magnificent act of self-sacrifice against hopeless odds made the enemy withdraw long enough to allow the large transport column to get clear unmolested, and to permit the evacuation of some of the wounded of his own platoon and of the light tanks.

Apart from the Welsh Guards, I could find no direct links between the Furness family and Wales, and the staff at the peerage section at Debrett's told me that they came from the Yorkshire and Durham area. They also told me that in the 1930s Lieutenant Furness's stepmother, the former Thelma Morgan, made headlines for a different reason. She was a mistress of the Prince of Wales who transferred his affection from her to Wallis Simpson, the American woman for whom he gave up his throne and title of King Edward VIII.

Wing Commander Hughie Edwal Edwards was serving in the Royal Australian Airforce when he won the Victoria Cross in 1941. He was born in Australia but there was enough Welsh blood in his veins for him to qualify to play rugby for Wales. His father Hugh, a blacksmith, lived at Pant-y-Fa Farm, Llwyn Gwril, Merionethshire. His mother was from Montgomeryshire. The family emigrated to Australia in 1909.

Wing Commander Edwards belonged to 105 Squadron and on 4 July 1941 he led a force of bombers, in daylight, at a height of about 50 feet through telephone wires and high-tension cables to attack the heavily defended port of Bremen in Germany. The bombers successfully penetrated fierce ack-ack fire and a dense balloon barrage, but further fire over the port itself resulted in the loss of four of the attacking force. His task completed, Wing Commander Edwards brought his remaining aircraft safely back, although all had been hit. He rose to the rank of Air Commodore in the Royal Australian Air Force.

Another RAF hero with Welsh connections was Flight Lieutenant David Lord, of Wrexham, who was awarded the Victoria Cross posthumously after being killed at Arnhem in the Second World War. Lord, who at one time studied for the priesthood at St Mary's College, Aberystwyth, was already the holder of the Distinguished Flying Cross. On the morning of 19 September 1944 he and other members of 271 Squadron RAF Transport Command left Down Ampney, Gloucestershire, to take vital supplies to Allied airborne troops trapped in the vicinity of the Dutch town of Arnhem. (The story of the battle for Arnhem is told in the blockbuster film *A Bridge Too Far*.) The 271 Squadron pilots were ordered to fly at 900 feet when dropping their containers.

Flight Lieutenant Lord's Dakota was hit twice by anti-aircraft fire and the starboard engine was set on fire when he was only minutes away from the dropping zone. He decided to continue with his mission, despite being targeted by a heavy barrage of anti-aircraft fire. His task completed, Lord ordered his crew to bail out. By this time the plane was down to 500 feet and burning furiously. There was only one survivor, Flying Officer Harry King, who was flung to safety.

For his actions David Lord was posthumously awarded the Victoria Cross. He is buried alongside his crew and the container dispatchers who were on his aircraft in the cemetery at Oosterbeek in Holland. David Lord is remembered on a memorial plaque at the Catholic Club in Wrexham. He was born on 18 October 1913 in Cork, Ireland, and before trying his vocation was educated at Lucknow Convent School in India and in Wrexham. He first flew DC3s with 31 Squadron, supply dropping in India, Egypt, Iraq, Libya and Burma. He was mentioned in dispatches for his long record of devotion to duty and in July 1943 was awarded the DFC. He was the only member of Transport Command to be awarded the VC. There is another tribute to him at the Battle of Britain Memorial Flight base at RAF Coningsby in Lincolnshire. It is a DC3 painted with the markings and in the colours of the Dakota flown by David Lord.

Another pilot in 271 Squadron was comedian Jimmy Edwards, the man with the traditional RAF moustache. He was awarded the DFC for exceptional flying on the Arnhem raid.

Wounded at Arnhem in a different incident was Tonyrefail-born Father Gerard Hiscoe, who was an army chaplain. After the war he was a curate at St Helen's,

Barry, and then went on to build the Church of the Blessed Sacrament at Goseinon, which is considered one of the finest modern churches in Britain.

DAM BUSTER

Wing Commander Guy Gibson VC, DSO, DFC of 617 Squadron fame was killed in action near Bergen-op-Zoom, Holland, on 19 September 1944, the same day as David Lord. Gibson, whose father came from Saundersfoot in Pembrokeshire, is buried at Steenbergen-en-Kruisland Roman Catholic cemetery, 25 miles south of Rotterdam. The previous year the 24-year-old bomber pilot was on leave in Penarth when he learned he had been awarded the VC for leading 617 Squadron in the Dam Busters raid on Germany on 17 May 1943. The following citation was published in the *London Gazette* in 1943.

Wing Commander Guy Gibson led the raid on the Mohne Dam, descending to within a few feet of the water and taking the full brunt of the enemy defences. He delivered his attack with great accuracy and afterwards circled very low for 30 minutes, drawing the enemy's fire on himself in order to leave as free a run as possible to the following aircraft. He then led the remainder of

Wing Commander Guy Gibson VC and his wife Eva.

his force to the Eder Dam where he repeated his tactics so that the attack could be successfully developed.

Nineteen RAF Lancaster bombers belonging to 617 Squadron took part in the raid on the Ruhr. The huge Mohne and Eder dams were breached by Barnes Wallis's bouncing bombs but two other attacks on the Sorpe and Schwelme dams failed.

I contacted Guy Gibson's widow Eva when researching the story of the blitz back in the 1960s. She wrote to tell me that she had decided to give no interviews, but I traced her sister, Miss Louise Moore, who was living in an old people's home in Penarth. She told me that Guy was in the audience at a Coventry theatre when Eve was dancing in the chorus of *Cat and the Fiddle*, and that is where they met. He courted her during the blitz on Coventry.

According to his logbook he flew from his air base in Lincolnshire to South Wales in a Blenheim aircraft for his wedding at All Saints' Church, Penarth, in November 1940. The newlyweds often visited Eva's parents, Mr and Mrs Ernest Moore, at their home in Archer Road, Penarth. Louise Moore said that Guy came to Penarth soon after the Dam Busters raid and there he received a call at his in-laws' house from Bomber Harris, the commander of Bomber Command, telling him that he had been awarded the Victoria Cross. Eve's father telephoned Penarth Golf Club and asked them to lay on drinks. The whole family went there to celebrate. It was a celebration tinged with sadness as glasses were raised to the memory of the fifty-three men who had died on the raid on the dams.

DAREDEVIL JACKSON FROM ST ATHAN

In May 2004 a Victoria Cross was sold for a record £235,000 at a London auction. It belonged to the late Sergeant Norman Jackson, one of 22,000 graduates from the engineering school at RAF St Athan in the Vale of Glamorgan. He was the only man connected with the base to win the VC. His citation tells his amazing story.

> On April 26, 1944 after bombing Schweinfurt, Germany, the Lancaster in which Sergeant Norman Jackson was flight engineer, was hit by an enemy fighter and fire broke out. Having asked permission to try to deal with it, Sergeant Jackson clipped on his parachute and, with a fire extinguisher, climbed on to the fuselage of the aircraft which was travelling at 200mph at 20,000ft. He tried to put out the fire, but his parachute partly opened and he slipped on to the wing. The fire spread and he was badly burned, then he was swept from the wing with his partly inflated, burning parachute trailing behind him. He landed heavily, breaking an ankle, and was taken prisoner.

He spent the rest of the war as a guest of the Germans, as did the rest of the Lancaster's crew after abandoning the burning aircraft.

After the war Norman Jackson was promoted to Warrant Officer. A total of 377 other St Athan flight engineers were awarded the DFC, DFM and other bravery awards during the war.

SPORTING GIANT

Maurice Joseph Turnbull, a major in the Welsh Guards, was killed in action in Normandy on Friday 3 August 1944. He was shot by a sniper and is buried in the war cemetery at Bayeux, the first town of importance to be liberated from the Germans after D-Day, 6 June 1944. He had married Elizabeth Brooke at Holy Souls Catholic Church, Scunthorpe, on 8 September 1939, just five days after war was declared. The couple had met at the Cardiff Squash Club.

Turnbull played cricket for Glamorgan and England and was capped as a goalkeeper for the Welsh hockey team and was also a squash champion. He was also one of six brothers who played rugby for Cardiff and in 1935 followed in his brother Bernard's footsteps to become scrum-half for Wales. He made his cricket debut for Glamorgan when he was only seventeen and still a schoolboy at Downside, near Bath. He went on to captain Cambridge University.

Maurice was secretary and captain of Glamorgan Cricket Club but also found time to be sports editor of the *Welsh Catholic Times*, which was launched in Cardiff in 1931.*

Maurice Turnbull's old school, Downside, was the scene of a tragedy that rocked Britain a few days before the last air raid on Cardiff in May 1943. A British military plane crashed on the playing field and killed nine members of the school's cricket team. The funeral of the boys took place at Downside on 19 May 1943, the day after the final raid on Cardiff.

Maurice Turnbull in the 1930s. *(Glamorgan County Cricket Club archives and Downside School)*

The boys were buried in the monks' graveyard at the famous abbey and school.

Wales has strong links with Downside. Dom Thomas Brown, the first post-reformation Catholic bishop appointed to the principality, was one of the founder members of the community that established the school. He was chosen for his role in Wales in 1840 after impressing the Vatican in the 1820s with his case for his Benedictine community to form a monastery at Downside after the Order was driven out of France.

* Turnbull's life story is told by Andrew Hignell in a fascinating book, *Turnbull, a Welsh Sporting Hero* (Tempus, 2001).

CODENAMED 'JANTZEN'

During late July and early August 1943, several ports and beaches around Carmarthen Bay played a vital role in a major logistical exercise under the direction of Western Command.*

Codenamed 'Jantzen', the exercise was enormous in scope and effort, and was planned with the utmost security. It was the first serious large-scale attempt to plan support for an army of invasion of German-occupied Europe.

Exercise Jantzen was not concerned with practising for the actual military invasion, but concentrated on the logistics of supporting such an operation and maintaining that support for approximately forty days. The main objectives were to plan the loading and unloading of essential supplies on short sea voyages. The maintenance of landing beaches was also a significant part of the exercise, as was the organisation of beaches for the efficient distribution of supplies. Important, too, was the construction of airstrips.

For two months before Jantzen began, many areas around Carmarthen Bay were visited by officers of Western Command. British, American and Canadian personnel visited docks and beaches at Port Talbot, Swansea, Llanelly, Ferryside, Llanstephan, Pendine and many other areas in Pembrokeshire, including Tenby, Saundersfoot, Wiseman's Bridge and Amroth. Civilians such as port authority and railway officials were also involved in the preliminary planning.

To simulate an invasion, some ports – including Port Talbot, Swansea and Tenby – were selected as 'friendly' areas from which support would be given to troops in 'enemy' areas such as Saundersfoot, which was selected as a bridgehead base of an Allied army of invasion. Amroth, with its shingle beach, was to be 'assaulted' and made into a maintenance area. Inland from Saundersfoot a substantial military base camp was established.

Exercise Jantzen did not call on large numbers of ground troops. The personnel involved were administrative staff, engineers, observers, signallers and salvage units. Simulated enemy attacks were made by the Home Guard and Polish Air Squadron No. 307 acted as the enemy air force. The Royal Engineers constructed an airstrip near Tavernspite, completing the task in less than 48 hours. There were also trials in the use of searchlights for night unloading and smokescreens as protection for vessels. The craft involved included twenty or thirty coastal steamers of between 800 and 1,500 tons, landing craft for both vehicles and personnel, ten concrete barges for transporting fuel and ten amphibious craft known as alligators.

During the exercise the weather ranged from calm to a Force 8 gale – the various climatic conditions that might be encountered in an actual invasion. Many of the routines were conducted successfully, but overall Jantzen was regarded as a failure,

---

* This amazing story was told to me by John Beynon, curator of Tenby Museum.

primarily because the concrete barges leaked, losing valuable petrol, which would be vital to the success of the real invasion. (One of these barges, later abandoned, served for many years as the landing stage at Caldey Island, home of a community of Cistercian monks.)

During the planning and execution of the exercise around the Carmarthen Bay area, strict security was in force throughout the beach and port areas and the surrounding countryside. A dawn-to-dusk curfew was imposed in Tenby from 12 July to 9 August 1943 and security checks were made on everyone travelling by rail and road into and out of the area. Civilians were not permitted to carry cameras, telescopes or binoculars, but local people took some surreptitious photographs. Some of those images are now in the Tenby Museum collection.

Everyone had to show identity cards on demand and from 27 June onwards all visitors to Tenby hotels had to register. Civilian mail, telephone calls and telegraph messages were subject to censorship. The harbour was cleared of all civilian boats prior to the start of the exercise. Apparently the tight security measures worked well and a test 'spy' sent into the area was soon apprehended.

Censorship of the press was evidently very successful too. The *Tenby Observer and District Reporter* for Friday 30 July 1943 – the height of the exercise – carried the headlines 'Thefts from the local laundry' and 'Fire guard schemes for the town as discussed by the Town Council'. Other front-page stories involved plans for a better water supply, which sat alongside an advertisement for the film showing at the South Beach Pavilion, *The Power and the Glory*.

Many Tenby people recall those days and remark on the intense speculation in the town: no one really knew what was happening. A popular view was that the invasion of Europe was about to take place and that Pembrokeshire ports and beaches were being prepared to receive thousands of fighting Allied troops.

There were rumours also that General Eisenhower, the Commander-in-Chief of Allied Forces, and Winston Churchill had been sighted in various parts of the area during the exercise. None was ever substantiated.

Jantzen may have been considered a failure, but it did, nevertheless, provide much experience, and many lessons were learnt that helped in the planning for the actual invasion of Normandy on D-Day, 6 June 1944. That operation, codenamed 'Overlord', was the greatest sea-borne invasion the world had ever seen. Overlord eventually led – despite enormous loss of life, including 1,500 Welsh soldiers – to the successful invasion of the European mainland, the first step in the eventual defeat of Germany. This successful outcome was due, in part, to the lessons learnt during that fourteen-day exercise in Carmarthen Bay during the summer of 1943.

There was no large-scale American military presence in Pembrokeshire during the exercise. American forces first came to the county in October 1943 when the 28th (Keystone) Division of the Pennsylvania National Guard arrived in the Tenby area.

Private Elwyn Edwards. *(Le Petit Journal)*

Commandos returning to HMS *Leopold* after the landing.

FIRST LANDING

Tuesday 6 June 1944 was the Longest Day, the day when the Allied troops invaded Normandy on the way to liberating continental Europe from the Germans. But the first landing of the war by British troops took place nearly three years earlier on 28 September 1941 and the only men to die were Welsh – Private Elwyn Edwards, a Welsh speaker from a farm near Ruthin, in Denbighshire, North Wales, and Lance-Corporal Cyril Evans from the steel town of Ebbw Vale, Gwent. Although they were not Catholics they are buried side by side in a Catholic churchyard in the village of Luc-sur-Mer in Normandy, the scene of the 1941 invasion.

Both men were among the 65-strong force that belonged to the Fifth Troop No. 1 Commando which took part in Operation Chopper-Deepcut, fifteen months after the fall of France. They were all volunteers and had trained in Scotland before sailing for France in HMS *Prince Leopold*, an adapted Belgian ferry boat. The Commandos left the ferry and boarded landing craft about 18 miles from the shores of Normandy. The object of the operation was to take prisoners and question them about the strength of the German garrisons in the area, with a view to a mass invasion. One group of Commandos landed at St-Vaast and engaged a German cycle patrol, killing two men and taking a wounded German prisoner. The second group landed at Luc-sur-Mer, a coastal village 10 miles north of Caen. Each Commando was armed with four Mills grenades and ampoules of chloroform, to put any prisoners they took to sleep. The Commandos retreated after coming under heavy fire at Luc-sur-Mer. Several were wounded, some, according to official records, by their own troops as the battle took place on a moonless autumn night.

The wounded prisoner taken at St-Vaast belonged to the German 183 Pioneer Battalion. He died on board the *Prince Leopold* as sixty-three of the invaders returned to Portsmouth, leaving the two Welshmen. Edwards (aged twenty) and Evans (twenty-four) died on the beach at Luc-sur-Mer, close to the hotel that the Germans used as their headquarters. The Germans gave them a full military funeral; their coffins were draped with Union flags and a volley of rifle shots was fired over the grave.

The secrecy surrounding the raid was such that it was not made public until a long time after the war. The families of the Welshmen who died were not told how they met their fate. The story was eventually revealed when Dr Len McDonnel, a nephew of Elwyn Edwards, investigated his uncle's death. McDonnel, a pathologist and cancer specialist in Ireland, was among a party of pilgrims, relatives, veterans and friends who attended a service at the Catholic church in Luc-sur-Mer in September 1991 to mark the fiftieth anniversary of the raid.

The villagers have cared for the graves of the Welsh soldiers since 1941 and a service is held annually at the church and at their graveside. There is also a memorial paying tribute to the Commandos on the seafront at Luc-sur-Mer. Among the pilgrims who went to the village in 1991 was John Iorwerth Davies, former chief librarian of Mid Glamorgan and a relative of Elwyn Edwards. Iorwerth provided me with invaluable documents and photographs. He said that Elwyn joined the Royal Welch Fusiliers before the war and volunteered for the Commandos. He was one of two adopted sons of Iorwerth's grandparents, John and Jane Hughes, of Plasnewydd Farm, Clawddnewydd, near Ruthin. The second adopted son, Herbert Jones, who lives in Denbighshire, also took part in the 1991 pilgrimage.

Cyril Evans enlisted with the Commandos from the 1st Brecknockshire Battalion of the South Wales Borderers. He was the son of John and Agnes May Evans of Cwm Ebbw Vale, Monmouthshire.

SECRET WEAPON

The Pembrokeshire coastal village of Angle played a key role in secret experiments in 1943, involving the bouncing bomb designer Barnes Wallis. A memorial to him and the bomb that was used in the Pembrokeshire experiment was unveiled at Withybush Airport, Haverfordwest, on 7 October 2003 – the sixtieth anniversary of Wallis's visit to the county. The unveiling was carried out by Wallis's son, also called Barnes.

The 1943 experiment took place six months after the Dam Busters raids in which 617 Squadron successfully used the bouncing bombs designed by Wallis. It tested a smaller version of the bomb in preparation for the invasion of Europe, which took place in June 1944. On 7 October 1943 Wallis was one of the VIP observers who saw a Mosquito aircraft, which had taken off from Angle, drop twelve small bouncing bombs, codenamed 'Highball', on a railway tunnel.

John Evans of the Pembrokeshire Aviation Group (PAG)* said Highballs were designed to target the Nazi railway transport system behind the front line in order to prevent German reinforcements from getting through. The plan was to bounce the bombs into tunnels to blow them up. Ron Dann, chairman of PAG, said that three of the bombs penetrated the tunnel. The explosives, dropped at 300mph, caused extensive damage during the test and broke up into pieces that scattered over a wide area. Fifty years later a member of PAG, John Gale, found a fragment of one of the bombs and it has now been mounted on a plaque which is on display at Withybush airfield.

It is believed that one of the reasons why the Highball was not used in action was that the concept was overtaken by another Wallis-designed bomb, the Tallboy, which was dropped from a huge height and burrowed into the ground before exploding. It was a Tallboy that sank the German battleship *Tirpitz* in 1944.

Barnes Wallis made a note of his 1943 visit to Pembrokeshire in his diaries, which are now deposited at the Yorkshire Air Museum. A large piece of a Highball bomb from Pembrokeshire has also been sent to the museum where there is a Barnes Wallis collection.

After the war the Maenclochog Tunnel was repaired and the line reopened, but it was closed for good in the 1950s. In the spring of 2004 the tunnel was still standing, albeit with a gap in the roof.

Earlier in the war the Maenclochog line in the Preseli Hills was used to test conventional bombs.

DUTCH COURAGE

If you are ever in Holland take time out to visit the historic town of 's-Hertogenbosch, known by locals as Den Bosch. There you will find one of the most impressive monuments to Welsh troops anywhere in the world, for the 53rd Division of the Welsh Regiment had its finest hours in this beautiful town on the left bank of the River Maas. Founded in the twelfth century, the town had been the scene of many battles throughout its history, but none greater than in the autumn of 1944 when the 53rd arrived to take on the Germans, led by General Friedrich Neumann.

---

* The aviation group was originally formed to set up memorials at various sites where aircraft, including three Liberators, crashed in Pembrokeshire during the war.

Commanded by Major-General Bobby Ross, the men of the 53rd were veterans of the fighting in Normandy and on the Dutch border. When the division arrived in Den Bosch on 19 October 1944, it and the East Lancs Regiment were tasked with liberating the town and cutting off vital supply lines for the Germans. The 53rd had the backing of tanks, crocodile flame-throwers and mine-clearing squads from other regiments. The Germans had no armour but thirty artillery guns, including eleven anti-tank weapons.

The first days of the battle were bloody and cruel with both sides losing many men. The division's progress was slow against the big guns of the Germans. In six days the 53rd suffered 123 fatal casualties, 75 men reported missing and 274 wounded. The British casualty roll for the battle was 144 (the same number of people who died in the Aberfan coal tip disaster in 1966).

53rd Division Memorial at 's-Hertogenbosch. *(O'Sullivan archives)*

The Dutch shared the pain in the battle for their town. A total of 180 residents, including members of the Resistance, died and 80 were severely wounded. All but three of the town's bridges were destroyed and not one building escaped damage. More than 700 premises were completely destroyed.

The town's magnificent cathedral survived without serious damage, even though the 53rd fired a staggering 89,932 artillery shells during the battle. The number of German casualties is not known but 1,700 men, including 2 regimental and 2 battalion commanders, were taken prisoner by the British.

The links between Wales and Den Bosch were forged in 1944 and remain strong today. The anniversary of the battle is always marked in the Dutch town on 27 October, when wreaths are laid on the memorial to the Welsh soldiers who died in 1944. The Pontypridd Branch of the Royal Regiment of Wales Association is now known as the Pontypridd/'s-Hertogenbosch Branch. An annual dinner is held to remember the men of the 53rd, the other regiments and the people of Den Bosch. Among the guests at the 2003 dinner at the Territorial Army Headquarters at Pontypridd was the deputy mayor of the Dutch town. It was also attended by just one survivor of the battle, Denis Welsh, a Chelsea Pensioner who had travelled from London for the occasion. During the weekend wreaths were laid at the regimental memorial at the Graig, Pontypridd.

AT REST AT LAST

The South Wales Borderers and Monmouthshire Regimental Museum in Brecon holds a Nazi flag that flew over the German Headquarters in Helmond, Holland, some 9½ miles east of Eindhoven. The flag was captured by 7 Platoon (A Company) of the 3rd Battalion the Monmouthshire Regiment when it cleared the town on 21 September 1944. The flag was personally signed by members of 7 Platoon and Company Headquarters personnel, including Company Sergeant Major Evan Davies from Abersychan, who was killed in action two months later at the age of twenty-seven. CSM Davies's body was not found until 2003; arrangements were made to re-inter him at Venray Commonwealth War Graves Cemetery in Holland, 25 miles east of Eindhoven. Retired Major Martin Everett, the curator of the regimental museum, told me Davies's remains were found near the castle (or Kasteel) of Broekhuizen in the Netherlands in February 2003 by a Dutch army recovery team. Their task is to find service personnel killed in the two world wars.

CSM Davies was killed in action in November 1944 during the attack on Broekhuizen. In 1944 and 1945 the 3rd Battalion was part of the 11th Armoured Division, which landed in France on 14 June 1944. The division reached Holland by September. By late November the Germans had been driven east of the River Maas except for a few pockets, one of which was at Broekhuizen where they held the village and nearby Kasteel – an old fort surrounded by a moat.

The infantry went in along a path cleared of mines by flail tanks. They had to cross 700 yards of open country and about halfway they came under withering fire. Scores of men, both company commanders and most of the other officers and senior NCOs were killed, including Sergeant Major Davies. The commanding officer, Lieutenant-Colonel Stockley, went forward on foot. He reached the forward troops, rallied the men and tried to lead a gallant attack on the Kasteel. He was killed, revolver in hand, leading his troops on the bridge over the moat.

The commanding officer of the 15th/19th Hussars went forward in his tank. A reserve company with only sixty men was ordered into the battle with tank support. They cleared the homes, which was no mean feat since there were more than 200 Germans in the village entrenched in a veritable maze of

Company Sergeant Major Evan Davies.

dugouts, trenches and reinforced houses. The Kasteel was attacked by tanks firing at point-blank range and then captured.

Victory had been obtained at a heavy cost. Of the 300 men who fought, 140 had fallen, including 10 officers, of whom 8 were killed. The bravery of these troops was recalled at the funeral of CSM Davies on 9 June 2004. His widow was eighty-six when she was told his remains had been found. She was too frail to attend the service in Holland but nieces and nephews were at the graveside, where the bearers and the honour guard were provided by the 1st Battalion the Royal Regiment of Wales, accompanied by the Brigade of Gurkhas' Band. As the 'Last Post' sounded and rifle shots were fired over the grave, another chapter in the history of the Second World War closed and a hero was laid to rest nearly sixty years after he died.

UNIQUE TRIBUTE

There is just one British soldier buried in the communal cemetery in the village of Kallo, a few miles to the west of the Belgian city of Antwerp. He was Aberfan-born Corporal Gwilym Brooks, whose grave is in a plot alongside Belgian Resistance fighters. The 38-year-old Welshman, the son of William Edward and Olivia Brooks, was a dispatch rider with the Queen's Royal West Surrey Regiment. Kallo claimed him as a hero after he helped the Resistance on 9 September 1944.

I met the leader of the Resistance fighters when I visited Kallo in 1964. He had fought alongside Welsh soldiers in the First World War and recognised Gwilym's accent. The Queen's Royals wanted to know if the Germans had left the village. The Resistance leader told me that the layout of the village was such that his group were finding it difficult to carry out a search. He continued:

Corporal Brooks volunteered to ride through the village on his motorbike. He managed to reach the end of the village without being stopped but on his return journey he was ambushed, dragged injured from his bike and left on the pavement outside the schoolmaster's house all night. The schoolmaster heard him being beaten

A relic from Kallo. *(O'Sullivan archives)*

and tortured and questioned throughout the night. He managed to pass him a drink of water but was unable to do anything else to help him. The brave Welshman died of his wounds the next day. We took what identity information we could from his uniform and buried him in our local cemetery. After the war the authorities wanted to remove the body and place it in one of the big war cemeteries in Belgium. We asked that it remain here. He died fighting for our village. He was one of ours. Kallo will never forget him.

And that is true. Services are held at the cemetery on the anniversary of Gwilym's death and the local children place flowers on his grave.

In the 1960s a group from the Royal British Legion in Aberdare visited Kallo and brought back the relics that had been taken from Gwilym's body. They presented them to his widow, Annie May Brooks, who lived in Miskin in the Cynon Valley.

ICY ORDEAL

Librarian Bryn Jones handled hundreds of queries in his role as head of the local studies section of Cardiff Central Library, but there are few stories to match the one involving a member of his own family: a Merchant Navy captain who came back from the dead.

Captain Danny Williams, Bryn's mother's first cousin, came from Cefn Cwrt Farm, near Llangrannog, Dyfed, where Welsh youth organisation The Urdd later established a camp. In 1942 Captain Williams was skipper of the *Chulmleigh*, a 5,550-ton tramp steamer owned by the Tatem Steam Navigation Company of Cardiff. It was his first command.

The vessel, with a crew of fifty-seven, set sail from Nova Scotia for Russia in November 1942 without an escort and with poor navigational aids. She was part of an experiment to test whether ships would be safer if they tried to reach Russia alone instead of in convoy. She was carrying 5,000 tons of army stores. In foul weather the *Chulmleigh* ran aground on an ice-covered reef off Spitzbergen's Spitj Cape. After failing to refloat the vessel the crew took to lifeboats, from which Captain Williams and the other survivors saw German Junkers 88s cripple the *Chulmleigh* with high-explosive bombs.

The lifeboats headed for the nearest known land, 150 miles away. A number of men died, including thirty-year-old Chief Steward John Islwyn Davies, who was killed by the freezing cold in the early hours of 10 November; his mates prayed as they slid his body into the sea. He was from Captain Williams's home county of Pembrokeshire and was the husband of Mildred M. Davies of Trefine. His name is recorded on panel 28 of the Tower Hill Memorial in London.

One of the lifeboats was lost with all hands, but Captain Williams and twenty-six of his crew were in the other lifeboat for six days. When the skipper collapsed and lost consciousness the third mate, twenty-year-old David Clarke, took charge of the situation. With grim determination and urging the men to muster strength from their frozen bodies, Clarke somehow got the lifeboat to Prince Charles Foreland off the Norwegian coast. It had a few primitive huts used by itinerant seal hunters in the summer season; one of these contained a stove and a quantity of coffee. In constant darkness the survivors of the *Chulmleigh* lived on the small amount of food they found in the huts and demolished some of the buildings to stoke the stove and keep warm.

Many of the men were suffering from frostbite and other injuries and after only four days thirteen had died of gangrenous septicaemia. There were only nine men left when the party was found on 3 January 1941 by two Norwegian soldiers from Barrentsburg, 12 miles from the place where the *Chulmleigh* crew had found refuge. The nine survivors were taken to Barrentsburg by a small fleet of sledges. During the fifty-three days of their icy ordeal the Germans launched two more aerial attacks on the crippled *Chulmleigh* and it was also torpedoed by a U-boat.

It took two months for the survivors to be nursed back to health before they could be returned to Britain. By then a memorial service for Captain Danny Williams and his men had been held at Capel y Wig in Llangrannog. Those attending the service on 20 December 1940 were convinced that no one had survived when the *Chulmleigh* was lost.

There was, of course, a great welcome for Captain Danny when he returned to Llangrannog in the spring of 1941, but there was one more amazing twist to the story. Danny's younger brother John was also in the Merchant Navy and was in the Middle East when he heard that the *Chulmleigh* had been lost with all hands. But as he walked along the quay one day he picked up a scrap of newspaper which included a report of his brother and eight other survivors being found alive. The scrap of newspaper stayed in John's wallet for the rest of his life.*

The story of the *Chulmleigh* was researched by Captain Danny's nephews Nick and Boyd Williams. They visited a museum at Longyearbyen in Norway where there is a section dedicated to the vessel. The exhibits include a pistol engraved with the name Captain Daniel Morley Williams. He gave the weapon to the soldiers who rescued him and his shipmates.

SHARK BAIT

One of the blackest periods in the history of sea warfare was recalled by Royal Navy veteran George Morgan. He was chief petty officer aboard the Kent Class heavy cruiser HMS *Cornwall* when it was sunk with the loss of more than 200 men by Japanese aircraft in the Indian Ocean on Easter Sunday, 5 April 1942. The *Cornwall*'s sister ship, HMS *Dorsetshire*, was sunk with the loss of even more lives in the same battle. Both ships went down in just 11 minutes.

---

* The invaluable help given to me by Bryn Jones at Cardiff Central Library has made my job as a journalist and historian so much easier.

Chief Petty Officer George Morgan (right) with one of his shipmates. *(Patricia Morgan)*

George, a non-swimmer, was twenty-two at the time. He was in the shark-infested, oil-covered sea for 30 hours before being rescued by a South African ship. He was one of more than 1,000 men from both ships who were saved. Newspaper reports of the time recorded the event. One from South Africa illustrated George's sense of humour despite the traumatic experience. He told a reporter, 'I was so covered in oil that I didn't sunburn at all!'

HAILED A HERO

First Wireless Operator Cyril George O'Keeffe was hailed a hero after sacrificing his life to save shipmates when their Merchant Navy vessel was hit by a torpedo fired from a German submarine on 9 January 1941. O'Keeffe, who was born in Cardiff in 1899, refused to leave his post and persisted in sending out a call for assistance. The SOS was picked up by a destroyer which rescued fifty-one sailors and five passengers who had taken to the lifeboats as the Hull steamer *Bassano* sank. When he knew that the destroyer was on the way O'Keefe jumped overboard to try to reach the lifeboats but drowned. He was the only man to die. His was the sort of deed that could have won the Victoria Cross had he been in one of the armed forces and not in the Merchant Navy. Surprisingly, he was not given any posthumous award, although his name is included on the Merchant Navy memorial on Tower Hill in London.

Cyril O'Keeffe had joined the Merchant Navy as a teenager; during the First World War the aerials on his ship were destroyed by a shot from a German submarine.

SS *SCILLIN*

More than 2,000 British prisoners of war died as a result of enemy ships being sunk by Allied submarines during the Second World War. The worst incident involved the Italian steamer SS *Scillin*, which was torpedoed by HMS *Sahib*. All but 24 of the British prisoners of war aboard the vessel died in the attack east of Tunisia. Only 36 of the 200 Italians on board survived the assault at around eight o'clock on 13 November 1942.

Colin Yaxley of the Manuscripts Department at the National Maritime Museum said a number of Welshmen, including members of the South Wales Borderers, were among those who died. It is believed that the prisoners were in the holds of the *Scillin* and had little chance of escaping.

The Bristol Channel paddle-steamer *Plinlimmon* (also known as the *Cambria*), which brought 900 men from Dunkirk to Margate. She was later used as an anti-aircraft vessel but was scrapped following a fire in 1946.

An internet site claims that historian Brian Sims – whose father was one of the prisoners killed – has found documents at the Public Record Office which show the Admiralty knew the vessel was carrying Allied prisoners. It says the Admiralty decided not to pass the intelligence on to Lieutenant T.H. Bromage, commander of the *Sahib*, because it wanted to protect the secret that the German Enigma codes had been broken at Bletchley Park in England. It was only in 1996 that the truth about the incident came out, and up until that time the prisoners' families had been told that they had died in Italian POW camps.

The submarine *Sahib* subsequently sunk the Italian transport ship *Galiola* off Sicily in April 1943, but came under attack from enemy ships and aircraft. The crew abandoned the submarine after it was holed by depth charges. One man was fatally wounded but the rest survived.

PADDLE POWER

For generations people living along the Welsh and English coasts of the Bristol Channel have got great joy out of boarding a paddle-steamer for a pleasure trip. At the beginning of the twenty-first century only one sea-going paddle-steamer remains operational. It is the *Waverley*, which has shared its time between the Bristol Channel, Scotland, London and the south-east coast of England for more than half a century. As old and new friends are introduced to the proud vessel, the role played by its sister ships in the Second World War should not be forgotten.

Twenty-five paddle-steamers took part in Operation 'Dynamo' when an armada of little ships evacuated 338,236 men, mainly British servicemen, from Dunkirk between 27 May and 4 June 1940. Six of the steamers were P. & A. Campbell vessels that had been used for pleasure trips across the Bristol Channel for decades. They were the *Devonia*, *Glen Avon*, *Glen Gower*, *Plinlimmon* (also known as the *Cambria*), *Snaefell* (which also used the name *Waverley*) and *Westward-Ho*. Two other Bristol Channel vessels also saw wartime service, the *Ravenwood* and the *Skiddaw* (also known as *Britannia*).

Not all survived the war. The *Devonia* was beached at Dunkirk after being crippled by German bombs.* The *Glen Avon* survived Dunkirk but foundered in a storm in 1944. The *Snaefell* also survived Dunkirk but was sunk in a bombing raid off Tyneside thirteen months later.

Signalman Leslie Rushleigh, who was in the Royal Naval Reserves, joined the *Devonia* at West Hartlepool on New Year's Day 1940. The vessel was on its way to the Firth of Clyde after being converted from a pleasure steamer to a minesweeper at Milford Haven. The thirty-seven crew members included twelve Maltese stokers from Cardiff and eight trawlermen from Hull and Stornaway.

One night in May 1940 Rushleigh received a signal ordering the *Devonia* to go to Tyneside then on to Harwich and eventually to Dunkirk. When the vessel reached the approaches to Dunkirk it was shelled and bombed by the Germans. The *Devonia* defended itself with a 12-pounder gun and a Lewis gun. It lowered some of its boats to bring servicemen from the beach to load them onto the Dutch coaster *Hilda*, which was manned by a Royal Navy lieutenant and three ratings. Then the *Devonia* was hit by a stick of bombs, which split open its stern. The order came to beach the paddle-steamer in the hope that it could be used as a pier for troops attempting to get to the fleet of rescue vessels, which ranged in size from small cruisers to destroyers. Bolstered by an extra ration of rum, the crew of the *Devonia* abandoned ship and rowed to the *Hilda* before transferring to the British destroyer *Scimitar*. The confidential papers aboard the *Devonia* were burnt by Signalman Rushleigh and the second engineer.

The *Glen Aron*, which operated in the Bristol Channel before the war, was off North Shields on Tyneside when the call came for it to join the rescue flotilla at Dunkirk. The vessel made two crossings from England to France and rescued a total of 888 men from the beach near La Panine. The *Glen Aron* was requisitioned by the Royal Navy in 1942 and was also used as a communications ship during the Normandy Landings of June 1944. After the war it returned to service as a pleasure cruiser in the Bristol Channel and operated there until it was decommissioned in 1960.

The *Snaefell*, which in peacetime went under the name *Waverley* in the Bristol Channel, managed to help another P. & A. Campbell ship, the *Glen Gower*, when

---

* The story of *Devonia* was told by one of its crew, Leslie Rushleigh, in *Paddle-Steamers at War*, an excellent book compiled by Russell Plummer, with the backing of the Chairman of the Paddle-Steamers Preservation Society, Terry Silvester, a Barry businessman. I am grateful for Mr Silvester's permission to use some of the information from the book.

it ran aground off Dunkirk. The *Gower* was towed into deep water. The *Snaefell* rescued 931 troops from the beaches in 1940, but was sunk off the River Tyne during an air raid on 5 July 1941. (There has been some confusion over the fate of P. & A. Campbell's *Waverley* because another paddle-steamer of that name, one owned by the London & North Eastern Railway Company, was sunk after being struck by German bombs while returning from Dunkirk. The Bristol Channel *Waverley*, sometimes known as the *Snaefell*, was the vessel lost off Tyneside in July 1941.)

The *Glen Gower* brought 1,235 troops back to Britain from Dunkirk in three crossings before it ran aground off La Panine carrying 500 soldiers and was towed to deep water by the *Snaefell*. In 1941 the *Glen Gower* was converted into an anti-aircraft vessel and it ended the war in the Scheldt Estuary.

The *Plinlimmon* (known as the *Cambria* when it operated in the Bristol Channel) completed one trip to Dunkirk, landing 900 men at Margate. It was not allowed to make further trips because of faulty equipment. The *Plinlimmon*'s crew relieved the exhausted men of the steamer *Oriole* on 3 June and made one more rescue trip. The *Plinlimmon* was converted to an accommodation ship in 1944 before being laid up at London Docks. It was gutted by fire and broken up in 1947.

By the time *Westward-Ho* reached the Dunkirk area from the Firth of Clyde the evacuation was well under way. The vessel rescued and landed 1,686 men, including a large French contingent. After Dunkirk the *Westward-Ho* returned to minesweeping duties before boiler trouble put it out of action. It finished the war as an accommodation ship at Dartford. It never returned to peacetime service and was broken up in 1946.

The *Ravenwood* returned to pleasure duties in the Bristol Channel from 1946 to 1954 after serving as an anti-aircraft vessel from 1942 to 1945. The *Skiddaw*, which operated in the Bristol Channel in peacetime as *Britannia*, carried out minesweeping duties until it was converted to anti-aircraft work in 1942. It returned to pleasure duties in the Channel from 1945 to 1956.

In 2003 the National Historic Ships Committee recognised the importance of the *Waverley*, the last sea-going paddle-steamer in the world. The ship, a frequent visitor to South Wales ports, was placed on the list of 'Designated Vessels'. This *Waverley* was built in 1947 to replace the one of the same name that was constructed in 1899, saw service in the First World War and was sunk off Tyneside in 1941. The new *Waverley*, the seventh to carry the name, is in good company on the schedule of historic ships, for among the seven vessels put on the list at the same meeting was the royal yacht *Britannia*.

ROYALS RESCUED

There are thousands of people who can tell individual stories about members of their families and I am privileged to be able to relate some of the deeds of my

A portrait of Leading Seaman Denis O'Sullivan by Jill Parkinson. *(O'Sullivan archives)*

father, Leading Seaman Denis O'Sullivan, affectionately known as Din.

He was on the destroyer HMS *Codrington*, the fastest ship in the Royal Navy which, before Din joined her, had cut her teeth patrolling the coast of Spain during the Spanish Civil War. He was on the *Codrington* in March 1940 when its job was to patrol the North Sea from Harwich. After being involved in the Battle of Narvik off Norway (see p. 83), the *Codrington* was ordered to Holland when the Germans launched their invasion of the Low Countries on 19 May 1940. Its job was to rescue the Dutch royal family and bring them to Britain.

As German paratroopers dropped from the sky near the port of IJmuiden, Din carried a young baby on board – she was Beatrice, the future Queen of the Netherlands. He used to joke that Prince Bernard had told the assembled crew that he would never forget the men of the *Codrington*, but 'The old bugger has never bought me a pint,' he said. Prince Bernard made up for this when he sent flowers to my mother May and Din on their fortieth and fiftieth wedding anniversaries.

The *Codrington* made eight trips to evacuate 5,821 troops from Dunkirk in May and June 1940. On 1 June the ship took Major-General Bernard Montgomery on a round-trip from Dover to Dunkirk. The destroyer was attacked by aircraft and shore batteries, but did not take one hit. Twelve days later the vessel helped to evacuate 11,000 troops from Le Havre.

Din later transferred to the cruiser *Engadine* and was severely wounded in action against the Japanese. He spent nearly two years in hospital in the United States and ended the war as a gardener and bodyguard to Admiral Binny, who lived in Dinas Powys before becoming Governor General of Tasmania after the war. Din overcame his war injuries to work as a docker at Barry, to care for myself, my sisters Pat and Elizabeth and brothers Denis, Michael and Peter. He died in the west wing of Cardiff Royal Infirmary in November 1989, shortly after his eightieth birthday. He made his last trip to sea when I took his ashes out in the Barry lifeboat to scatter them around the Marker Buoy. My mother died at the age of eighty-five at Llandough Hospital in July 1996.

THETIS LOST

In June 1939 a newly launched submarine failed to resurface in Liverpool Bay just hours after leaving the shipbuilding yard at Birkenhead. All but 4 of more than 100 sailors and civilian technicians died in the tragedy. The 4 survivors reached safety by using Davies apparatus and surfacing through the escape hatch.

Initial attempts to raise the vessel were abandoned but four months later the *Thetis* was raised to aid Britain's war effort. The submarine was towed to and beached at Traeth Bychan, near Moelfre, Anglesey. Ninety-nine entombed men were recovered and taken for burial at Holyhead. The submarine was refitted and renamed *Thunderbolt*. She served in the Mediterranean with distinction until she was sunk during enemy action off Sicily in 1943.

LIFEBOAT HEROES

Lifeboats around the coast of Wales were manned by older men throughout the war as their younger colleagues were inevitably in the armed forces, usually the Royal or Merchant Navy. An incident involving the Canadian frigate *Chebogue* in October 1944 resulted in William Gammon, Coxswain of the Mumbles lifeboat, being awarded the RNLI's Gold Medal for bravery.

Lifeboat Coxswain William Gammon. *(RNLI Archives)*

The story of the *Chebogue* is told by Charmion Chaplin-Thomas on a Royal Canadian Navy website. He recorded that on 4 October 1944 the frigate was torpedoed by German U-boat 1223, commanded by Oberleutnant Friedrich Altmeier. The Canadian ship was part of a convoy sailing from Liverpool to Halifax in Nova Scotia. The attack took place in the North Atlantic, nearly 900 miles west of Ireland. An acoustic torpedo blew off much of *Chebogue*'s stern, killing seven men, badly injuring several more and carrying away the vessel's propellers. The other ships of the group rallied around to pick up the dead and injured, a dangerous business as the submarine was still in the area. Listing and helpless, *Chebogue* began to drift, her silhouette sharply illuminated by the full moon. Damage-control parties went to work in the frigate, and by 1 p.m. the next day she was watertight and stable enough to be towed to the nearest haven – Wales.

A number of ships took it in turns to tow the crippled frigate 890 miles to Swansea Bay, where deteriorating weather forced her to run aground on Port Talbot Bar. The RNLI Press Office took up the story from here. All telephone lines had been brought down but a messenger alerted the Mumbles lifeboat crew, two of whose members were over seventy years of age. They were old enough to remember an incident forty-one years earlier when the Mumbles lifeboat had capsized on the Port Talbot Bar, killing six of the eight crew members. On the stormy night in October 1944 the lifeboat *Edward, Prince of Wales* was launched at Mumbles and ploughed in the dark through rough seas to reach the crippled warship.

Coxswain Gammon decided that the only way to get close to the vessel was to head shorewards into the surf, steer round the grounded stern before turning into the storm and back out to sea, pausing a few seconds alongside the frigate on the way. Twelve times the lifeboat carried out this dangerous manoeuvre to allow forty-two Canadians to leap from their ship onto the Mumbles vessel. One second the lifeboat was level with the men gathered on the deck of the frigate and the next she had been plunged up to 20 feet below them by the waves. Three or four men jumped to the safety of the lifeboat each time. One man broke a leg, a second landed on top of Coxswain Gammon, badly bruising the Mumbles man, and a third fell into the sea, but was pulled aboard the lifeboat by Gammon. The lifeboat landed the forty-two rescued sailors safely ashore. Coxswain Gammon was awarded the RNLI Gold Medal, his mechanic William Davies and bowman Thomas Ace were awarded RNLI Bronze Medals.

Sadly, on 23 August 1947 Gammon and Davies were among eight lifeboatmen who lost their lives when the *Edward, Prince of Wales* overturned while going to the aid of the crippled steamer *Samptampa*.

The *Chebogue* incident was far from the only rescue carried out by Mumbles crews between 1939 and 1945. The Second World War was only thirty-three days old when Mumbles lifeboatmen were called into action. The reserve vessel, the *J.B. Proudfoot*, was launched on 6 October 1939 after the Royal Mail Lines motor vessel *Lochgoil*, sailing from Newport to Vancouver, hit a mine 5 miles from the Scarweather lightship. The *Proudfoot* rescued forty-two passengers. The Cardiff steamer *Philip M* took the twenty-two crew members on board.

At 9.15 a.m. on 21 January 1940 Swansea coastguards reported a vessel sinking about 6 miles off Mumbles Head. The *Prometheus*, from Liverpool, had hit a mine. A Royal Navy patrol vessel rescued fifty-three people and the Mumbles lifeboat took twenty-two others to safety. On 7 February 1940 Coxswain William Davies was given the RNLI Vellum of Thanks for his part in rescuing thirty-seven men from the steamship *Eldonpark* of Greenock, which ran aground at Port Eynon. The crew was all crowded into the wheelhouse, the only part of the steamship above water when the lifeboat arrived. On 29 February 1941, during the height of the Swansea blitz, the Mumbles lifeboat went out to the steamship *Fort Medine*, which had struck a mine in the Bristol Channel. There were no survivors.

The *Elizabeth Elson* from Angle in Pembrokeshire was in the front line of the battle against Germany. The RNLI's records show that her first wartime call came on 18 September 1939, when the search for the crew of a crashed aircraft ended without success. On 10 October 1940 the lifeboat rescued four sailors from the motor vessel *Alderney Queen*, which was sunk by a German aircraft north-west of Skokholm Island. On 26 March 1941 the large cable-laying steamer *Faraday* was bombed and set on fire 3 miles from St Ann's Head. The Angle lifeboat went out to meet a Belgian trawler which had some of the *Faraday*'s crew on board and others in tow in their own boats. The lifeboat collected the fifty-six survivors and landed them safely.

Many of the calls off North Wales were to crashed British or German aircraft, but more often than not the aircrews were dead. The feelings of the lifeboatmen were summed up by the Holyhead Coxswain Matthews who said: 'I'd rather go a hundred times for nothing but disappointment, than once have a life lost for want of me being there.' Matthews and two of his crew, Richard Evans and Robert Williams, were decorated after rescuing the crew of a Whitley bomber in perilous conditions in the Irish Sea.

DANISH TRAGEDY

A brief report in the *South Wales Echo* of 7 April 1942 put me on the trail of a tragic story relating to an incident in my home town of Barry. The report told of an explosion and fire aboard an unnamed ship which entered a South Wales port on 6 April – wartime censorship had prevented the vessel's identity from being disclosed.

The story reminded me of a report published many years later about Phyl Wells, who had looked after many of the 103 war graves in Barry cemetery since 1948. They included the graves of 6 Danish Merchant Navy seamen who were killed on 6 April 1942. Four of the men had died when an explosion occurred aboard the Danish ship *Soborg* as it was entering Barry. The other two men, who were among eight seriously injured, died in hospital. The incident happened when some of the crew were cleaning a gun. Three doctors were taken out to

Phyl Wells was awarded the MBE for looking after the graves of Danish seamen and in May 2004 I had the privilege of joining Phyl (seventy-eight) and her eighty-year-old husband John at the memorial to the Danish sailors. John, who served in the RAF during the war, was engineer on the Barry lifeboat for thirty-two years. *(John O'Sullivan)*

the burning vessel where members of the crew not affected by the explosion worked heroically to recover their dead and injured shipmates. The ship was berthed at the docks where the fire was brought under control by local firemen. The Danish seamen who died were A.J. Arrenhius, A. Bruno Frederiksen, Sven Hansen, D.A. Herskind, A.O. Gorgensen and M. Kruse.

Barry is one of only a few ports in Britain to be licensed for handling explosives. After the war the dockers there handled ammunition, loading it onto old vessels which were towed out into the Atlantic and sunk.

HISTORY CHANGED

Bob Wyer, a scrap car dealer whose yard was near Cardiff Airport, helped change history by his actions during the war: he saved the life of a pilot, and that pilot was Ian Smith, the man whose Unilateral Declaration of Independence in the 1960s took Rhodesia – later named Zimbabwe – out of the British Commonwealth.

The Rhodesian was the pilot of a fighter plane that caught fire after crash landing on an RAF base in the Middle East. Bob Wyer, who was one of the ground crew, braved the flames to release Smith and carry him to safety seconds before the aircraft exploded.

They talked again for the first time in 1985 in a radio interview. During their two-way chat, with BBC Wales presenter Martin Williams in the chair, Ian Smith, who was no longer Prime Minister, was full of praise for Bob Wyer. He admitted that had the rescue failed, the history of Rhodesia would probably have been much different. 'It took guts to get me out of that burning plane and I have never forgotten you,' Smith told Wyer, who modestly said he was only doing his job. During the interview former Prime Minister Smith also said that he had played rugby for Llanelli Stars while stationed in Pembrokeshire during the war.

Bob Wyer hit the headlines in the 1980s when he won jackpots in the same week on both Littlewoods and Vernons football pools. Sadly he was terminally ill at the time and didn't live long to enjoy his £1.5 million windfall, but he threw a party at the Six Bells, Penmark, for the nurses and medical staff who had been looking after him.

130 SORTIES

In April 1942 the Distinguished Flying Cross was awarded to Flying Officer John Arthur Jarvis of Llandaff, Cardiff, who by the age of twenty-seven, had flown 130 sorties against the Italians, including day and night bombing operations. He had also carried out low-level attacks against enemy ground targets in Greece.

On the same honours list, Flying Officer Ivor Broom, whose address was given only as Glamorgan, was also awarded the DFC. He had completed forty-five sorties with 107 Squadron and among the targets he hit was a 400-ton ship, which was set on fire and sank.

Around the same time wireless operator Sergeant Evan David Fowler, a former lathe operator from Abercynon, was awarded the Distinguished Conduct Medal after his aircraft was forced down in the sea. He spent 15 hours in a dinghy before being rescued. Warrant Officer B.D. Lewis, a former tinplate worker from Abercarn, was awarded the Distinguished Flying Medal for constant service since joining the RAF in 1934.

KILLED IN THE LONDON BLITZ

A prominent Welshmen, Sir Vyvyan Cory, was injured when the famous London night club, the Café de Paris, was bombed on 8 March 1941. He died in Charing Cross Hospital nine days later. The 33-year-old special constable had succeeded to the barony of Coryton when his father died in 1935. He was the grandson of Sir Herbert Cory, the 1st Baron of Coryton, Whitchurch, Cardiff. The *South Wales Echo* carried this vivid account of the incident:

> Women in evening dress and officers in uniform figured prominently among the couples crowding the dance floor, moving to the rhythm of Ken Snakehips Johnson and his West Indian orchestra just before two bomb hit the Café de Paris. The dancers made their way to their tables, corks popped, glasses tinkled and excitement increased. In a few minutes the cabaret would begin. The perfumed atmosphere was warm and friendly. The war was a long way off.
>
> A second later it had crashed into their midst. A bomb, tearing through the roof, exploded with a terrific report on a balcony immediately above the orchestra. Debris was hurled in all directions, causing death and further destruction. The gay throng, literally hurled to the floor by the blast, were lying everywhere – some dead, many more injured, and the more fortunate only dazed.

Snakehips Johnson, most of his orchestra, and M. Poulson the famous restaurateur, were killed. A staircase leading from balcony to dance floor was wrecked. Ceiling decorations had been ripped away to add to the avalanche of debris from which members of the band struggled to escape. Flying fragments of wine bottles and glasses were responsible for many injuries and a number of victims staggered to the street bleeding freely from cuts.

Prominent among the helpers was a young nurse from Chelsea who was off duty and a young Dutch member of the Fleet Air Arm. Between them they attended to many of the injured and were also instrumental in getting other nurses rushed to the scene by taxi. The cabaret girls escaped the force of the explosion and a number of staff in the foyer of the café helped in the rescue work.

Sir Vyvyan Cory's name is recorded in the Westminster Book of Remembrance.

One of Britain's greatest jockeys and trainers, Wrexham-born Fulke Walwyn, and his wife Catherine were also at the nightclub but escaped unhurt. Racing expert and author Brian Lee said that Walwyn won the Grand National on Reynoldstown in 1936. He also won five Cheltenham Gold Cups, six Hennessy Cups, seven Whitbread Gold Cups, five King George V Boxing Day races and two Champion Hurdles. After being injured in a fall at Ludlow in 1938 he became a trainer at Lambourne and trained more than 2,000 winners, including an incredible 200 at Cheltenham. The owners he worked for included Queen Elizabeth the Queen Mother. Walwyn's father, Colonel Fulke Walwyn, was based in Abergavenny and was the Master of the Monmouthshire Hunt. Walwyn junior made his mark in point-to-point racing before winning his first race on Alpine Hut at Ely Racecourse, Cardiff, in the early 1930s. He was leading amateur rider on three occasions. He died in 1991.

Another leading Welshman who died in the London blitz was 77-year-old Lieutenant-Colonel John Evans Lloyd, who was High Sheriff of Anglesey in 1935.

He was killed when a bomb hit his home in Eleanor Road, Brentwood, on 12 March 1941. Colonel Evans Lloyd was chairman of the Monmouthshire brewery firm of Webbs (Aberbeeg) Ltd. During the First World War he commanded the 9th Battalion King's Liverpool Regiment in France.

JEWISH MEMORIAL

At least twenty-five members of the Cardiff Jewish community were killed in action during the Second World War. A memorial to these men was unveiled at the Cathedral Road Synagogue in 1951 and the order of service included a photograph and pen picture of each of the victims. It is a unique document – most war memorials carry only the names of those lost and not where or how they died – but the experiences and bravery of these men echo the experiences and bravery of thousands of other Welshmen of all faiths.

The document tells how Major R. Stuppel of the Royal Army Medical Corps was captured by Germans at Tobruk and escaped but was then recaptured south of El Alamein. He escaped again, this time from Naples to Switzerland, but was recaptured by Italians at the border. He then escaped from a transit camp in Austria, reached Yugoslavia and fought with the partisans under Marshal Tito. He was killed in action on 31 October 1943. It also lists the following:

RAF Flight Engineer L. Bassman (22) was co-pilot of a plane that crashed on landing while returning from a bombing raid on a submarine base in Norway on 4 October 1944.

Captain P.M. Bogod (22) was awarded his pilot's wings in 1942 and killed on active service on 19 May 1943.

Lieutenant P. Clompus (21) of the Royal Armoured Corps was killed while leading an attack on Fortuna Ridge in Tunisia on 18 September 1944.

Royal Navy Chief Petty Officer David Cowen (31) served on the aircraft carrier HMS *Dasher* in the Pacific, on the Russian convoy route in the North Atlantic and off Norway. He was killed in an explosion aboard the *Dasher* in the Firth of Clyde on 27 March 1943.

Sergeant Air Gunner D. Davies (21) flew twenty-eight operations, and although wounded refused to be grounded. He died while bombing Aachen on the night of 24/25 May 1944.

RAF Sergeant S. Felman (23) flew at least fifteen operations before his plane was brought down over the East Friesian Islands on 10 April 1941. He is buried at Leer.

Corporal E. Fine (33) of the Royal Army Service Corps served in Java, Burma, the Dutch East Indies and Singapore before the ship he was on was torpedoed in June 1945.

RAF Corporal C.H. Goldman (24) died at RAF Innsworth Hospital, Gloucester, in January 1943.

RAF Corporal A. Grunis (26) was taken prisoner in the Far East and was a prisoner of war in Java. He was being transferred from one camp to another in a Japanese ship when it was sunk on 29 November 1943.

RAF Sergeant Air Gunner T. Hazan (21) was shot down over the Mediterranean on 23 June 1942.

Radiographer Sergeant W. Hollman of the Royal Army Medical Corps was killed in Haifa, Palestine, on 6 February 1940.

Merchant Seaman H. Huntman (25) was reported missing, presumed dead, on his first trip in July 1940.

Welsh Guardsman S. Huntman (25) took part in the Anzio landings in Italy and was killed at Montecassino, Italy, on 11 February 1944.

Captain J.H. Joseph RMC (26) was killed at Cleve, Germany, on 9 March 1945.

RAF Flight Sergeant H. Levene (34) was killed over Belgium in 1943.

RAF Flight Sergeant H.K. Levy (25) lost his life over the Aegean Sea near Greece on 6 November 1943.

Merchant Navy Steward S. Messer (26) was killed on 2 December 1940 aboard the *Lady Glanely,* which sailed from Cardiff Docks.

RAF Sergeant Air Gunner S. Miar (25) flew 147 day hours and 167 night hours during twenty-two flights over France, Holland, Germany, North Africa and the Middle East. He was presumed killed on 13 April 1941.

Able Seaman C. Newman (22) was taking part in the evacuation of Crete when his ship, HMS *Glenroy,* was sunk, but he survived. His next vessel was torpedoed while running supplies to the 8th Army. On 11 May 1941 during the Battle of Malta his third ship struck a mine and went down with the loss of all hands.

Royal Navy Stoker J. Phillips (26) was lost at sea in May 1943.

Royal Navy Steward J. Phillips (19) was lost at sea in June 1941.

Merchant Navy Steward L. Phillips (17) drowned at sea on 17 December 1944 while serving on SS *Isbjon.*

Glider pilot Sergeant T.A. Rubenstein, Army Air Corps, was killed at Arnhem on 22 September 1944 on his last flight before taking up ground duties.

RAF Sergeant Air Gunner E. Shatz (23) was killed over France on 16 March 1944.

THE MAN WHO NEVER WAS

There are strong suggestions that a South Wales man was at the centre of the intriguing mystery of 'the man who never was'. The book and film of that name tell the true story of a body that was released from a British submarine in 1943 and washed up on a Spanish beach. The dead man was carrying documents that falsely identified him as Marine Major William Martin from Cardiff. He was also carrying confidential papers. The Spanish authorities handed the documents over to the Germans who, as a result, were misled into believing that the Allies had abandoned plans to invade Sicily and would target Greece instead. German troops were moved from Sicily and consequently thousands of lives were saved when the invasion took place there.

But who was 'Major Martin'? One theory is that the body was that of Emlyn Howells, who died in Paddington General Hospital in London in 1943 from bronchial pneumonia after suffering long-term tuberculosis. Author James Rusbridger claimed in his book *The Intelligence Game* (published by Bodley Head in 1980) that Howells's body was used to fool the Germans.

Most of the research was by Colin Gibson, a former Pontypridd policeman. He was 110 per cent certain that Emlyn Howells was the man buried in Spain. However, he traced a headstone for an Emlyn Howells in Treorchy Cemetery. This man was born in 1887 and died in January 1943. The body in Treorchy was exhumed and the authorities claimed that it was definitely that of Howells. Then documents made available at the Public Record Office in the late 1990s named 'the man who never was' as Glyndwr Michael, a tramp who came from Wales and who committed suicide in 1943. But new doubts were thrown on this in a television documentary aired in October 2003. The programme suggested that the body could be that of Able Seaman Thomas Joseph Martin, a 24-year-old from Wandsworth Common, London. He was one of a number of seamen who died in an explosion aboard the Royal Navy aircraft carrier HMS *Dasher* on 27 March 1943. The incident took place in the Firth of Clyde, not far from where the submarine set off for the coast of Spain just a few days later. This makes sense as it was important that the body should convince the Spanish authorities that the man had recently died of drowning. Able Seaman Tom Martin's grave is said to be at Ardrossan Cemetery in Scotland, and is marked with a headstone on which his name is carved. Perhaps this grave, like that of Emlyn Howells, should be exhumed to establish the truth.

But perhaps the body was not that of Emlyn Howells, Glyndwr Michael or Tom Martin, but another victim of the incident aboard HMS *Dasher*. A Cardiff man, David Cowen (thirty-one), also died in the explosion and his death adds to the mystery. According to a document published for the unveiling of the Jewish Memorial at the Synagogue, Cathedral Road, Cardiff, after the war, Cowen was a Royal Navy chief petty officer who had served on HMS *Dasher* in the Pacific, on the Russian convoy route, in the North Atlantic and off Norway before being killed in the explosion in the Firth of Clyde on 27 March 1943. His rank and name are on the Jewish War Memorial in the Cardiff Synagogue, but there is no Chief Petty Officer Cowen listed in the Commonwealth Graves Commission's records. A David Cowen who died in the explosion on HMS *Dasher* is commemorated at Chatham Naval Memorial in Kent, but he is listed as a canteen manager with the Royal Naval Canteen Service and not as a chief petty officer. Even more intriguingly, there is no record of his last resting place. If the theory about someone from HMS *Dasher* being used as a decoy is right, could David Cowen of Cardiff have been the posthumous hero who saved thousands of lives after his own death? Was it a coincidence that the body washed up on the Spanish beach carried papers claiming that the man was a native of Cardiff? It is a question that may never be answered unless the secret files are opened to the public.

SCARLET AND BLACK

A priest from South Wales helped to run the Vatican escape line for Allied prisoners during the Second World War.

The operation was led by Monsignor Hugh O'Flaherty, an Irish priest who became known as the Scarlet Pimpernel because of the many disguises he used to trick the Germans and the Fascists. His story was told in the blockbuster film *The Scarlet and Black* (1983) and he was assisted by Newport-born Father Tom Lenane.

Lenane was based at the Rosminian House in Rome during the war, avoided prison himself by taking the identity of a dead Irish priest and forging a passport, with the help of a stamp he carved from the heel of a shoe. It was the first of many passports he produced to help Allied servicemen on the run from the Axis powers.

In the 1960s one of the escapees, Lieutenant Charles Wyatt from Mayfield in Sussex, was a surprise guest of honour when the former Prime Minister of Ireland Sean Lemass opened St Mary's Social Club at Newport. Mr Lemass came at the invitation of Father Lenane, who was then rector of the parish.

Charles Wyatt, an Anglican, said he had sought help at the Collegio Missionaria Antonio Rosmini in Rome after escaping from an Italian prisoner-of-war camp where he had been kept since being captured in North Africa:

> Father Tom even fooled me that he was an Irishman and he gave me a brilliantly forged passport which had originally belonged to Father Patrick Fox who died in Rome in 1943. Father Tom also fitted me out as a priest and gave me instructions as to how I should behave so as not to make the enemy suspicious.
>
> I attended Mass and took part in other religious ceremonies, one of which gave me the fright of my life. It was All Souls' Day, November 2, and I accompanied Father Tom and other members of the household on a visit to a cemetery to pray for the dead, including Father Fox, the man who I was posing as. It was a public cemetery and scores of German Catholic soldiers were there praying for their dead and I feared that I would make a mistake and give the game away at any moment.

On one occasion Father Lenane was forced around the mission house at gunpoint and arrested and questioned by the police, who rightly suspected that he was helping Communists and Jews, an offence for which he could have been executed. But that was not his only worry. Father Lenane told me with that famous twinkle in his eyes, 'I was more concerned about Charles Wyatt eyeing the Italian girls while he was dressed as a priest. That would have given the game away more than anything else!'

FLYING PULPIT

Anglican minister Bill Winton was an army chaplain at Dunkirk and he went to war in his 'flying pulpit', a battered Austin Seven, which covered hundreds of miles in

France and Belgium before the evacuation from Dunkirk in June 1940.* He left the car, engine still running, in a forest a few miles from the Dunkirk beach where thousands of men were waiting to be repatriated to Britain.

Bill Winton had gone to France with the British Expeditionary Force in September 1939. Their job was to strengthen the defences on the frontier between France and Belgium in preparation for a German invasion. But it was not to be. The so-called 'phoney war' ended in the spring of 1940 when the Germans crashed through the Maginot Line. Their tanks and armoured cars crushed buildings and people

Padre Bill Winton.

alike as they pushed forward, and the British Expeditionary Force had to evacuate.

When he reached the beach at Dunkirk, Bill had plenty to do. He treated the wounded, comforted the frightened and prayed for the dying. On 3 June 1940 he and some of his regiment boarded a destroyer which brought them back to England. Padre Bill survived to continue his work as a chaplain.

Later he was parish priest at St Mary's Anglican Church in Whitchurch, Cardiff. We talked about many things over a pint in the Royal British Legion, where he was chaplain, but he didn't much want to discuss the horrors of war.

In April 1941 the *South Wales Echo* reported that an unsigned message in a bottle had been found on the foreshore at Port Talbot. It was dated May 1940 and read:

> We are just two lads in khaki and as I write this note the boys of the British Army are fighting for their lives on the sandy beaches of Dunkirk. Though we may never see our native land again it is good to know that we have done our best for our country. Cymru am byth [Wales for ever].

The bottle was found by a Mr E. Dixon of Greenfield Cottages, Abercregan, Port Talbot.

BACKBONE OF THE AIR FORCE

It was in June 1936 that the Air Ministry bought seven farms in the Eglwys Brewis area of the Vale of Glamorgan in preparation for building a major base that would wing into action in the event of war. The name of Eglwys Brewis was dropped in favour of St Athan because of the challenge of pronunciation.

---

* This story was told in the *South Wales Echo* in the 1960s by feature writer Peter Tate.

It was decided that in addition to its role in storing aircraft, St Athan would be a training station, and the construction workers who moved there in 1937 were to build thirty-six hangars. In addition twenty small storage sheds were added at various points around the perimeter of the airfield. Work also started on a military hospital and on a 4,000-foot runway.

On 1 September 1938 the advance party of twenty-five airmen arrived at St Athan from RAF Henlow and were given the job of preparing billets. They had arrived at Gileston railway station carrying their own rations and had to lay out the dining-room before it could be used. By the middle of October there were more than 1,000 airmen on the camp, which was to become one of the biggest in the world. Some training aircraft were brought in to add a touch of authenticity to the base where an Astra cinema, a large dance hall and gymnasium, three churches, a swimming pool, a large roller skating rink and a NAAFI were established.

When war was declared on 3 September 1939 St Athan's buildings were sandbagged, parts of the canteen and main stores were turned into anti-gas centres, trenches were dug and defensive positions established. About 900 more men arrived at the camp, followed by another 400 four days later. They were given a fast-track course in servicing aircraft and working on Rolls-Royce, Kestrel, Merlin and Bristol Pegasus engines.

In January 1941 virtually everyone on the camp was given unexpected leave when a big freeze did what the Germans failed to do – put the base out of action, cutting off the electricity and water supplies. The personnel were told to go home 'and we'll send for you when we need you!'

When the base was fully operational it was training up to 5,000 airmen at a time, with some 500 moving out to begin practical work on the fighters that helped win the Battle of Britain and the bombers that carried out raids on Germany. Those being trained at St Athan included Free French Air Force cadets as well as ground crews from Belgium, Czechoslovakia, Norway and Poland. Later in the war American troops were stationed nearby and Italian prisoners of war were attached to the base.

Official records show that between 1941 and 1951 some 22,599 flight engineers were trained at St Athan, the vast majority of them during the war years. A former St Athan trainee, Sergeant Norman Jackson of 106 Squadron, was awarded the VC for his bravery (see p. 92). A total of 377 other St Athan flight engineers were awarded the DFC, DFM and other bravery awards during the war.

LADY ROWENA'S FURY

Lady Rowena Traherne, whose husband Sir Cennydd Traherne became Lord Lieutenant of Glamorgan, didn't think much of Göring's Luftwaffe. She was working at St Athan Military Hospital when a lone Heinkel bomber dropped a stick of four bombs on 18 July 1940, killing one man and damaging the old sick quarters at Eglwys Brewis, which then housed the infectious disease wards. Lady Rowena was also at the hospital on 24 August 1940 when six high-explosive bombs landed in or near the building. There were no serious casualties but there was considerable structural damage. After the raid, Lady Rowena told friends:

> On a quiet evening in August a lone German plane came over Glamorgan and stupidly dropped all its little 250lb bombs on our hospital. We were all furious. They fell all over the place, the medical wards were worst hit but only one man was slightly injured. He was in the WC and the water cistern – the high-level type – fell on his shoulder. Sister Fluffy Jones – later Mrs Iris Bower – was on duty and was excellent, encouraging everyone and cheering on her night staff, of which I was lucky to be one.

Sister Fluffy Jones had been touring the hospital with a Red Cross volunteer nurse when the raid started. Sister Jones later recalled in a booklet recording the history of the hospital:

> Suddenly we heard the sound of bombs dropping with no warning given at all. The Germans had beaten the sirens to it. I heard Nurse Traherne shouting don't run. In a few seconds I had reached a ward of patients and found the entrance had vanished. It was pitch black and some were shouting, rushing water could be heard. Suddenly I seemed to be falling into a deep hole and realised it was a bomb crater. I climbed out pretty fast and the first patient I came to was still sitting on a lavatory, all the wall had disappeared. I could see by the light of my torch that blood was streaming down his face. He was shocked but by some miracle was not badly hurt. We could see the funny side of the situation that he was still sitting on the loo. We reached some of the

Lady Traherne.

other patients who were in some distress. Fortunately most had only minor injuries, because their wards were built of timber and there was no heavy masonry.

Doctors, nurses and medical orderlies started evacuating the hospital – patients were taken to Whitchurch, Llandough and hospitals in Cardiff. The ghostly figures running about, the ambulances coming and going made it a hectic scene. For her leadership that night, Fluffy Jones was presented with the Royal Red Cross Medal by King George VI at an investiture at Buckingham Palace in February 1941. She later went to the cinema and saw a newsreel of herself leaving the palace. Fluffy's war didn't end there. She was one of the first two paramedics to land on the Normandy beaches seven days after D-Day.

In November 1943 a burns treatment unit was opened at St Athan to care for British bomber crews who had been wounded in action and the rebuilt hospital played a key role caring for the wounded repatriated from France after D-Day. Patients of many nationalities were admitted, and by late 1944 all 330 beds were occupied. The records show that one patient from southern Texas was able to speak to his sister who had telephoned to check on his condition.

One of the first WAAF officers to be posted to the hospital was Susan Williams MBE, who later became Lord Lieutenant for South Glamorgan. She recalled the hard life of the nurses: among numerous rules governing their lives were the requirements that they needed a pass if they expected to be off the station after 10 p.m. and that they always wear white sleeves at meal times. 'The station commander was not mad about having women on the station,' she said.

After the war the hospital continued to serve the area, dealing with both military and civilian patients. It closed on 28 December 1961.

MIGHTIER THAN THE SWORD

South Wales Echo cartoonist J.C. Walker proved that the pen was mightier than the sword with his timely and hard-hitting illustrations both before and during the war. In the 1930s the Fascists were growing in strength and popularity, not only in Germany, Italy and Spain, but even in Wales, where there were active groups of Blackshirts. One Cardiff group tried to hijack a ship to sail to Spain to fight on the side of the dictator Franco.

But J.C., who had fought in the First World War, reduced Hitler and Mussolini to figures of fun – clowns in the international circus. Some of his cartoons published at the time that Italy invaded Abyssinia in 1935 so infuriated the Italians that their consul in Cardiff called on the lord mayor at the City Hall and demanded that the cartoonist be put in prison or even shot for insulting Mussolini. The lord mayor sent him packing, reminding him that Britain was still a free country with a free press.

J.C. Walker, Bisley marksman and cartoonist.

From the *South Wales Echo* on Armistice Day, 11 November 1939. The caption read: 'It should have been her 21st Birthday Party.'

In August 1939, when hostilities seemed inevitable, J.C. depicted a minute Hitler beside the wheel of a huge war machine. Hitler was telling the driving instructor that he could see the pedal for starting, but he didn't know where the pedal was for stopping. The instructor told him there wasn't one. War was declared on Sunday 3 September 1939. The night before, J.C.'s cartoon had shown Hitler as a burglar breaking into a window marked Poland. Watching him was a British bulldog.

The cartoon of 25 October 1938 showed Ribbentrop – who was then the German Ambassador to Britain – describing Britain as a toothless lion. J.C.'s update on the theme a year later showed a worried-looking Ribbentrop calling Britain a vicious animal that must be destroyed.

The British government didn't escape J.C.'s broadsides. On 28 September 1939 he depicted a British 'IOU-boat' with the commander's eye on tobacco tax, surtax, beer tax, whisky tax, income tax and even sugar tax. The government came under fire from J.C. again on 31 October 1939 when he featured a 'Red Tape Concentration Camp', showing the atrocities of rising petrol prices, coal rationing, restriction on shopkeepers and blackout regulations.

In a November 1939 cartoon J.C. depicted the propagandist William Joyce (known as Lord Haw-Haw) as 'Lord He-Haw', with the head of an ass. Walker may well have met Joyce in the 1930s, as the traitor lived in Colum Road, Cardiff, and also in Barry. But J.C.'s most poignant cartoon appeared in the *Echo* on 11 November 1939 – Armistice Day. It showed the 'Peace Angel' in prison, tethered by a ball and chain marked with a Swastika. The caption read: 'It should have been her 21st Birthday Party.'

When he retired, J.C. moved to England. He died at his home in Barley, Hertfordshire, on 24 October 1981.

FLOATING HARBOUR

Jim Hennessy MBE was a larger-than-life character, who combined determination with integrity, compassion, generosity and love for his family. He was also one of Cardiff's most successful businessmen and he played a key role in the D-Day landings in the Second World War.

It was in 1944 that the Admiralty turned to Mr Hennessy's company in Cardiff to build large tank components for the Mulberry floating harbours that aided the Allies when they invaded France. The company also helped the war effort by making smoke bombs, air ducting, mine flaying equipment and armoured plate structures.

Mr Hennessy set up the City Welding Company after becoming one of the first people in Britain to be trained in carbon arc welding. His company was a training school for welders who helped to build 1,000-gallon steel oil tanks and a vast range of other products.

Mr Hennessy, who also founded the Fairholme Caravan Company in Cardiff, died on 8 June 2003, a few months short of his ninetieth birthday. He had a great

Sportsman David Winter.

love of music, was the uncle of folk singer Frank Hennessy and a former president of the Cardiff Male Choir.

AN INSPIRATION TO PEOPLE WITH A DISABILITY

Rookwood Hospital in Cardiff cared for wounded servicemen, many of whom had lost limbs in action. The bravery of the patients was matched only by the devotion of the staff who looked after them. There are legendary stories of how severely wounded men helped each other to and from the pubs in Llandaff where they enjoyed the company of the regulars and a good pint of Brains beer. There are many tales that can be told about the men who came back from the war with

125

wounds that destroyed their normal life. One of those men was David Winter, who was a patient at Rookwood for more than fifty years.

He was one of the greatest sportsmen Wales has ever produced, although wheelchair-bound from the time he was paralysed by a German shell in 1944 while fighting in France after D-Day. Once he came to terms with his injuries David became a pioneer in the world of paraplegic sports, and his courage and determination encouraged hundreds of people with disabilities to test their skills at a variety of activities.

David Winter was in his early twenties when the shell injured him for life. Initially he found it very difficult to accept that he would spend the rest of his life in a wheelchair, but the Port Talbot-born hero started rebuilding his life at Rookwood. First as a patient and then as an occupational therapist, he lived at the hospital for more than five decades.

His first foray into competitive sport was in the early 1950s when he started making his mark in sabre fencing. He went on to win more than 160 medals in fencing, archery and bowls. At the Paralympic Games in 1968 he won gold in sabre fencing, and went on to represent Wales at fencing and archery in four Commonwealth Paraplegic Games and Great Britain in three Paralympics. He also competed at the European Games. The softly spoken man whose mild-mannered way contrasted with his determination and aggression as a sportsman, graduated in 1973 from a competitor to a full member of the Sports Council of Wales, taking the place of Olympic gold medallist long jumper Lynn Davies.

As an administrator David Winter attended the Paralympics in Rome, Tokyo and Israel. In 1974 he was appointed an MBE – an honour he considered to be a tribute to all the organisers and competitors in the Paralympic Games.

As David Winter made clear to anyone who listened, his injury was no real impediment. Despite living most of his adult life in hospital he probably did more, travelled more and met more people than he would have done had he not been injured in battle.

When Winter died at the age of seventy-three Howard Jones, Director of the Wales Council for the Disabled, said that this remarkable man had inspired hundreds of disabled people throughout the world.

HUNDREDS INTERNED

In the spring of 1940 Italians in Swansea held a festival in a parish hall decorated with a photograph of Mussolini (who didn't take Italy into the war on the side of the Axis until some months later). When Italy's neutrality ended hundreds of Italian men in Wales were picked up in dawn raids and taken to internment camps.*

---

* Their story is told in *Alien Land* (G. Ronald, 1961) by Jack Parker, a former *South Wales Echo* journalist.

THE WELSH AT WAR

In 1984 Mario Basini, a feature writer with the *Western Mail*, told how some, including his father, were sent to the Isle of Man. Others were shipped to Australia or Canada, and 700 did not make it. They were on a Canada-bound ship that was torpedoed by a German U-boat only two days out of Liverpool. Among those who died was Mario's uncle, his mother's youngest brother.

Near Newcastle Emlyn, Dyfed, there is a fascinating relic of the Second World War, the Nissen hut that was used as a site to hold Mass by the Italian prisoners of war. There are faded religious paintings on the wall and Spam tins, which were used to hold candles. Some of the former prisoners returned there in the 1980s when Mass was said in the hut which had meant so much to them in the 1940s.

When Mussolini was captured and executed by Italian partisans his body and that of his mistress were hung upside down on a lamppost. The photograph of the gruesome scene was published on the front pages of newspapers in Allied countries. The photographer, who was serving in the British army at the time, was Ron Bevan of Aberdare who, as a freelance, took many photographs for the *South Wales Echo* and *Western Mail* in the 1960s.

CAVALRY CHARGE

A Second World War hero who survived the German concentration camps died in Cardiff in May 1980. He was Dr Josef Wienlawa-Klimaszewski, and his body was taken back to Poland to be buried near his parents and brother in Poznan. As an officer in the Polish cavalry Dr Klimaszewski took part in what became known as the last organised cavalry charge in history. Armed with belts of Molotov cocktails the horsemen charged German tanks and achieved considerable success for a number of hours before fighter planes and bombers brought an end to the encounter.

Dr Klimaszewski was taken prisoner but escaped and joined the Polish Free Army, which was re-formed in Persia by the British Eighth Army. He served under Field Marshal Bernard Montgomery in North Africa and Italy and won the Polish equivalent of the Victoria Cross.

An expert in international law, he opted to come to Britain in 1947, but like other displaced persons had to work as a labourer, unloading fish at Cardiff Docks. His training as a lawyer enabled him to help many immigrant families throughout Europe, although he eventually used his talents in the business world, becoming managing director of the building firm DMD. With this company he was involved in building the Empire Pool, the South Stand of the National Stadium and the UWIST building in Cathays Park, all in Cardiff.

Another Pole, Madame Helena O'Rourke Brochocka (a niece of the former Bishop of Danzig, Count Edward O'Rourke), and her three children were refugees at Chepstow during the Second World War. The family had escaped from Poland via Lithuania.

The Polish line of the O'Rourkes came from those who left Ireland after the Battle of the Boyne in 1690. They served in the French army, and were given the title of count by Louis XV. They went to Russia in the eighteenth century, served in the Russian army High Command and obtained the Russian title of count. General Joseph O'Rourke, who won fame during the Turkish and Napoleonic Wars, married a lady of the Polish aristocracy in about 1810 and bought large estates in Poland.

MALTESE BROADCASTS

Michael Camilleri acted as unofficial Maltese consul in Cardiff from 1918 until his death in 1964. When the Second World War started he was on holiday in Malta with his family but arrangements were made for him to return to Cardiff immediately because of his status in the city. When Malta was under siege, Michael's morale-boosting broadcasts were relayed by the BBC from Cardiff to his homeland. He later ran the George Cross Club in Cardiff and raised thousands of pounds for Maltese charities.

A Welshman also played a vital role during the siege of Malta: HMS *Welshman*, a Manxman corvette minesweeper and one of the fastest ships in the Royal Navy. HMS *Welshman* supported the island of Malta during the long siege in 1942 and early 1943. The island's population resisted strongly and was collectively awarded the highest decoration for civilian bravery, the George Cross. *Welshman* dodged the German air and sea defences many times to take ammunition, spare parts for Spitfires, oil and food to the island. On one trip she landed Vice-Admiral Payne, who was appointed as commander-in-chief of the forces in Malta. When she was berthed in Valetta Harbour the vessel suffered a near miss which put one of her three engines out of commission, seriously affecting her speed. However, she made it home to the United Kingdom and was repaired at Devonport. She then returned to the Mediterranean.

HMS *Welshman* was returning from Malta to Alexandria when she was sunk by German U-boat 617 on 1 February 1943. Very few of the 148 crew survived. The people of Malta saluted the *Welshman*, which brought them hope and supplies and helped the island and the British troops based there eventually to beat the Germans.

EIN TAD YR HWN WYT YN Y NEFOEDD

Visitors to the Holy Land may have wondered how a Welsh-language version of the Lord's Prayer came to be placed on the wall of the Church of the Pater Noster in Jerusalem. Arthur Jones, who comes from Carmarthen, provided the answer in the 1970s.

He was in the RAF and was one of the Welsh servicemen who thought it only right that the language of the angels should be included among other world languages at the famous church. They approached Richard Hughes, who was chairman of the Welsh Society in Jerusalem during the Second World War, and he contacted the Urdd headquarters at Aberystwyth. The young people of Wales responded magnificently with donations of money and stamps. A craftsman in Jerusalem made the plaque, enabling Welsh speakers to join in the most precious of prayers at the very spot where Jesus first spoke the words to his disciples: 'Our Father who art in Heaven . . . Ein Tad yr hwn wyt yn y Nefoedd'.

MEMORIES OF A MONASTERY

A relative of a British officer who was based at a monastery in Belgium just before Dunkirk was traced in Cardiff. Letters written to Lieutenant Charles Sweeney of the 2nd Battalion of the Royal Ulster Rifles were found by the monks at the Abbey of Our Lady of Saint Sixt in Westvleteren, near the Belgium–French border. He left the letters behind when his unit, including General Montgomery, fled the abbey to reach the coast to be evacuated to Britain in advance of the German army in June 1940. An appeal made in the *South Wales Echo* led to Lieutenant Sweeney's sister Eirene Parfitt, one of the writers of the letters in April 1940. She said that he had died in a car crash in Germany after VE Day.

A MAN TO BE FEARED

Most people's view of the Home Guard has probably been influenced by Captain Mainwaring, the bumbling bank manager who led the Warminster-on-Sea platoon in the popular television series *Dad's Army*. But at Ebbw Vale the real-life situation was so much different. The captain of the Home Guard there was the most decorated non-commissioned Welsh soldier of all time. He was John Henry Williams, a commissioner at the steelworks until shortly before his death on 7 March 1953.

On his Home Guard uniform he wore the ribbons of the Victoria Cross, the Distinguished Conduct Medal, the Military Medal and Bar, the 1914–15 Star, the British War Medal, the Victory Medal and a French honour, the *Medaille Militaire*, which is the equivalent of the Victoria Cross. The awards to the then Company Sergeant Major John (Jack) Henry Williams were for outstanding action during the First World War. He was also awarded a George VI Coronation Medal.

Jack Williams was born in Nantyglo, Monmouthshire, in 1886 and quit his job as a colliery blacksmith to enlist in the 10th South Wales Borderers in November 1914. He was promoted to sergeant in January 1915. He was awarded the Distinguished Conduct Medal for continued and sustained coolness and gallantry during the Battle of Mametz Wood from 10 to 12 July 1916. He got the Military Medal for bravery at the beginning of the battle for Passchendaele heights at Pilkem Ridge on 31 July 1917. He was awarded a Bar to his Military Medal for bravery during a raid near Armentières, where he brought back a wounded comrade on 30 October 1917. He earned the Victoria Cross less than five weeks before the Armistice was signed in 1918. The citation for his VC was published in the *London Gazette* on 14 December that year:

> For most conspicuous bravery, initiative and devotion to duty on the night of 7th–8th October 1918, during the attack on Villers-Outreaux, when, observing that his company was suffering heavy casualties from an enemy machine gun, he ordered a Lewis Gun to engage it, and went forward, under heavy fire, to the flank of the enemy post which he rushed single handed, capturing fifteen of the enemy.
>
> These prisoners, realising that Williams was alone, turned on him and one of them gripped his rifle. He succeeded in breaking away and bayoneting five enemy, whereupon the remainder again surrendered. By this gallant action and total disregard for personal danger, he was the means of enabling not only his own company but also those on the flanks to advance.

Company Sergeant Major Williams received the VC, DCM, MM and Bar from King George V at Buckingham Palace. It was the first time that the king had decorated the same man four times in one day. At the time of the investiture the Nantyglo man was still recovering from severe wounds sustained during the battle in which he won the VC. During the ceremony the wound in his arm opened up and he had to be given medical treatment before he left the palace. CSM Williams had been medically discharged from the army on 17 October 1918 after being severely wounded by shrapnel in the right arm and leg, but it seems likely that he would have been more than a match for the Germans had they parachuted into Ebbw Vale during the Second World War.

Ironically the only action involving the Home Guard at Ebbw Vale, recorded by local historian Gerry Jones, could have provided a first-class episode of *Dad's Army*. In October 1941 the Ebbw Vale platoon was mustered at 4 a.m. one morning after reports that German parachutists had landed on the Domen Fawr mountain. When they arrived at the scene the Home Guard found that the invaders were two small balloons used for weather forecasting.

Jack Williams is not forgotten in Ebbw Vale. There is a memorial plaque to him in the Civic Offices there. He was employed for a while as a rent collector but was more at home in the uniform of a commissioner at the general office of the steelworks. In 1924 he was chosen to hand a wreath to the then Duke of York (who was later crowned George VI) at the Newport Cenotaph. Five years later the Ebbw Vale hero represented the 10th Battalion (First Gwent) South Wales Borderers at the unveiling of the memorial to the 24th Regiment South Wales Borderers at Gheluvelt, near Ypres in Belgium.

OLDEST SURVIVOR

The oldest survivor of the Battle of the Atlantic was 88-year-old Mrs Charlotte Pugh of Hamilton Street, Mountain Ash. She was on a merchant ship, not named because of wartime censorship, which was sunk in 1942. She was returning from Australia where she had been staying with her daughter since the autumn of 1939. She was on the outward voyage when war was declared. Her son-in-law was named Osborne and he was a police constable at Mountain Ash before emigrating to Australia.

TAFF SWIMMERS KILLED

A man who carved a name for himself as a swimmer in Cardiff was killed in action in the spring of 1942. Cecil Deane won the Taff Swim in Cardiff five times during the 1930s and was a great favourite with the crowds who lined the river at Cardiff for the races, sponsored by the *Western Mail and Echo*. A member of the Penguin Swimming Club, London, Deane came second to Derek Powell of Newport in the 1939 race, which took place just weeks before war was declared.

Another Taff swimmer who died during the war was Gordon Williams, a brilliant young commercial artist who was killed while serving with the RAF in southern Rhodesia (now Zimbabwe) in 1944. His brother, Eric Williams, is one of the most respected businessmen in Cardiff. Their father started the first hairdressing salon in the city.

GRAVE MISTAKE

In a churchyard near the Cefn Mably Arms, between Cardiff and Newport, there is a grave which some history books wrongly link with Deputy Führer Rudolph Hess, who was number three in the Nazi hierarchy, behind only Hitler and Herman Göring.

Hess put on a Luftwaffe uniform and flew a German fighter plane alone towards Scotland on what he described as a peace mission. The flight took place on 10 May 1941, just before the Nazi invasion of the Soviet Union. Hess intended to see the Duke of Hamilton, whom he had met briefly during the Berlin Olympics in 1936. With extra fuel tanks installed on the Messerschmitt Me110, Hess made the 5-hour, 900-mile flight across the North Sea and managed to land within 30 miles of the duke's residence near Glasgow, Scotland. He was captured by a farmer.

When the story broke in the national press, the Mackie family in Michaelston-y-Fedw in Gwent claimed that a late relative of theirs was the first wife of Rudolph Hess's father, Carl Hess. The woman was Elizabeth Mackie, who was born in the village and who was buried in the Cefn Mably churchyard. She did marry a Carl Hess, who at one point worked at Ely Hospital, in Cardiff.

The more I visited the grave the greater my doubts about the story became, so I wrote to Rudolph Hess's son when he was on a visit to Britain. I had a reply on his behalf from the German Embassy in London. The letter revealed that the Carl

Hess who worked in Cardiff was not a member of the top Nazi's family and the grave was not connected with Rudolph Hess, who was born in Alexandria, Egypt on 26 April 1894. He was the son of a prosperous wholesaler and exporter, not a humble hospital porter. Rudolph Hess did not live in Germany until he was fourteen. After serving in the First World War he joined the Nazi Party on 1 July 1920, becoming the sixteenth member.

Rudolph Hess did visit Cefn Mably after landing in Britain, however. He was interrogated at Cefn Mably Hospital, which was an intelligence base. Hess displayed signs of mental instability to his British captors and they concluded he was half mad and represented only himself, not Hitler and the Third Reich. Churchill ordered that Hess be imprisoned for the duration and treated like any high-ranking prisoner of war. Hess was also declared insane by Hitler, and effectively disowned by the Nazis who were embarrassed by his actions.

He was detained at Maindiff Court Hospital, Abergavenny, where he apparently displayed a paranoid obsession that his food was being poisoned. His only friend at Abergavenny was an aggressive white swan that he used to feed when he was allowed to go under escort on visits to White Castle.

In 1945 Hess was returned to Germany to stand trial before the international military tribunal at Nüremberg, where one of the court shorthand writers was Bert Michelle, City Hall correspondent on the *Western Mail* (and a former colleague of mine). Hess was sentenced to life in prison. The Soviets blocked all attempts at securing his early release from Spandau Prison, Berlin, where he committed suicide in 1987 at the age of ninety-two, the last of the prisoners tried at Nüremberg.

LUMBERJILLS

An insight into what life was like in the Land Army was given by Lyn Price (née Ceaton) in an interview with the *South Wales Echo* in the 1980s. When she was just eighteen, Lyn left her job selling shoes in a Cardiff store to become one of thirty-two Land Army girls who formed the South Wales contingent of the Women's Timber Corps. As a Lumberjill she worked in the Swansea Valley from 1943 to 1945 – swinging a 14lb sledgehammer and 7lb axe as well as any man.

'We would be up to our knees in a bog, traipsing through snow and ice and we'd have to walk two or three miles in chrome boots to get to work,' recalled Lyn. 'Blisters and aching muscles were all part of the job, so were stomach muscles that got so hard that we would have difficulty having children. When I had my daughter a doctor described my stomach muscles as like a brick and told me he would rather deal with a woman who sat in a chair knitting all day than someone who had been as active as I was.'

When the Lumberjills, who included clerks, shop assistants and hairdressers, turned up at local dances the band would salute them with the popular number 'The Woodchoppers' Ball'. The Lumberjills were felling trees to provide wood for pit props and railway sleepers; the rest was burnt as fuel or used to help make nylon or gas masks. The girls were paid 21s a week, out of which they had to buy their own working clothes, for which they had to use their clothing coupons, leaving very little for an off-duty wardrobe. There was a bonus for the girls – because they were doing manual work they were allowed an extra ounce of cheese with their weekly rations.

Rationing was one of the biggest problems for people throughout Britain. It was introduced in 1939 and continued until July 1954. The weekly allowance for each person included 4oz

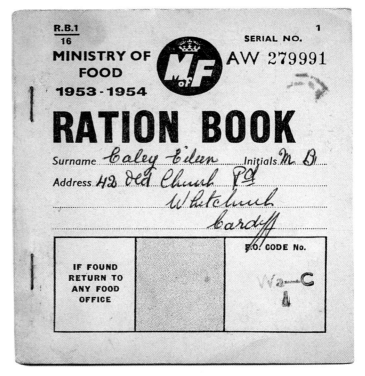

Ration books were used up to 1954. This one belonged to author John O'Sullivan's late wife Eileen (née Caley).

butter, 2oz margarine, a shilling's worth of meat for each adult and half that amount for each child. Jam, marmalade, syrup and sweets were rationed and most people were restricted to just 1oz cheese a week. The only exceptions were agricultural workers, miners and vegetarians, who were allowed 8oz cheese. Protests from grocers that 1oz cheese was too small for them to measure fell on deaf ears.

WALDINI'S WAR

Waldini went to war armed with a cello and leading a troop of seventeen musicians and dancers.

The Good Companions Concert Party from South Wales was formed by Waldini, Cardiff's own Wally Bishop who started entertaining troops while serving with the 53rd Division of the Welsh Regiment in the Middle East during the First World War. At forty-five he was too old to return to the colours when war broke out in 1939 but was quickly signed up for ENSA (the Entertainments National Service Association) by band leader Jack Hylton.

Waldini's orchestra and concert party played at RAF camps in the early days of the war but later entertained front-line troops in the Western Desert, Tunisia and

Sapper Ron Bishop with his father, Waldini, at Catania.
(From *Front Line Theatre*)

Sicily. In his biography *Front Line Theatre*, Waldini told of concerts on a troop ship on the way to Algiers:

The stage was rigged up on the after hatch. In front was a sea of faces stretching along our deck as far as the upper decks, and above that an ocean of faces looking down on us. Others had perched themselves anywhere it was possible to hang on and get a view. High up on the gun platform, a solitary gunner divided his attention 'twixt the danger that lurked above and the concert ready to start below.

As we made our way to the stage and the girls in their pretty gypsy costumes climbed on, a roar of approval went up – and another roar when a playful sea-breeze frolicked round a flimsy dress, revealing a shapely leg. The show commenced! Every voice joined in the popular tunes we were now playing like 'Don't Sit Under the Apple Tree with Anyone Else but Me.'

Waldini said there were tears when Phyllis (he didn't mention her second name) sang 'Where E'er You Walk'.

Soft-hearted tough men, shedders of tears one moment, killers of men the next. Men who, on bended knees before battle, pray for courage, and in it curse the One who died for them! Men who hate their officers like poison on the parade square, and yet will go through hell with them in battle.

The show concluded with Elaine playing her accordion for the community singing. Everyone joined in with 'Song of Twilight' and linked hands for 'Auld Lang Syne'.

The men went to war. Waldini and his entertainers followed them. As he followed Monty's Eighth Army, the Desert Rats, Waldini caught up with the news from home, from a seven-week-old edition of the *South Wales Echo*.

The more you thought about it the more you realised what newspapers stood for to the men in the front line. It was the missus putting the coal on the fire; the kid sister running in from school shouting is dinner ready, Mam? The pot boiling on the hob and the cat purring on the mat. And much more too! Yes it was home . . . really HOME.

Later on the tour, the Companions put on a show at a field hospital, where more than 1,000 wounded soldiers were being cared for.

With a leg missing or an empty sleeve, men sing with such feeling as to put the entertainers' own troubles in the shade. Brenda's high kicks and splits, the lovely curves that are good to see. But when a soldier's sight is missing. . . . When Phyllis sang there were men who couldn't hear her. Their eardrums had been shattered by the noise of battle.

In Catania the Good Companions had a guest artist, the legendary Gracie Fields, who sang a melody of songs, including 'The Biggest Aspidistra in the World' and 'Sally'. She finished by singing the Lord's Prayer.

After arriving in the Middle East, Waldini had one prayer, to meet up with his son Ron who was in the Eighth Army. The band leader was just finishing a meal with Gracie Fields when a voice said, 'Hello, Pop.' It was Ron, who was in a field hospital recovering from wounds.

The Good Companions followed the Eighth Army to Sicily and Italy before the concert party was posted to India and Burma, returning to Britain in time to join in the victory celebrations. Waldini returned to Cardiff and his Gypsy Band played at local dance halls where he was often approached by ex-soldiers who thanked him for the ENSA concerts.

I got to know Waldini well, and even played the accordion with his band on one occasion. In the 1960s he was a drinking pal of *Echo* news editor Walter Grossey. We reporters took it in turns to collect Walter from the Park Hotel and often joined him, Jack Key, who was manager of the Odeon cinema, and Waldini for a drink in the American Bar.

BLAZE AWAY

Wearing their black and gold uniforms, the Madam Collins Rosita Accordion Band and Concert Party helped to keep South Wales smiling throughout the Second World War. The group staged concerts in Merchant Navy clubs and on military camps, in church halls and chapels and even in cinemas. Their signature tune,

'Blaze Away', was as well known in Barry as any wartime song, but most members of the concert party were hardly old enough to know the rude words sung to the rousing tune of 'Colonel Bogey'!

The accordionists, singers and dancers rehearsed behind the blacked-out windows of a former shop in Main Street, Cadoxton, Barry. Madam Gladys Collins was a strict teacher who demanded – and got – the best out of her pupils, most of whom obtained high marks in music examinations. But the discipline of the music room was forgotten when the air raids came and we kids took our squeeze boxes into the shelters to help keep up morale. My sister Pat and myself and some cousins and neighbours were all members of the band and I remember playing in Harvey Street, Cadoxton, when Ernie Holding came home safely from Dunkirk.

There were house parties to entertain soldiers, sailors and airmen billeted in Cadoxton and concerts for wounded servicemen in local hospitals. Accordion music rang out in the streets on VE Day as we celebrated the end of the war. And more than 1,000 people crowded into the old Plaza cinema in Cadoxton for a 'Welcome Home' concert to raise money to honour the heroes arriving back from the battle front or prisoner-of-war camps.

Mind you, not everyone enjoys the accordion. My brother Denis quotes Oscar Wilde who declared that a gentleman is one who knows how to play the accordion – but doesn't. Denis is convinced that had the Allies played the accordion over the German airwaves instead of bombing German cities, Hitler would have waved the white flag years earlier.

SCHOOLGIRL HEROINE

Margaret Vaughan was only four when the Second World War started and grew up, like all of that generation, in a South Wales under attack or threat of attack from German aircraft. She lived in Shirley Road, Plasnewydd, Cardiff, and her house was damaged by bomb blasts when the Albany Road area was targeted on 3 September 1940.

Margaret's father was a policeman based at the Home Office headquarters in Coryton, Cardiff. He and his wife thought it best that Margaret go to live with her grandparents in Abergavenny, where she stayed for fifteen months before returning to live in Westfield Road, Whitchurch, close to where landmines landed on the Philog and in Pantbach Road.

She survived the war, and when she was only fourteen and still a pupil at Penarth County School, having moved there from Glanynant School, Whitchurch, she became the youngest female holder of one of the country's highest bravery awards. In 1949 she was given the Albert Medal (in 1971 this award was converted to the George Cross), the highest honour bestowed on civilians.

On 28 May 1949 Margaret was enjoying a day out at Swanbridge, a beach between Penarth and Barry. A group of Boy Scouts had left it too late to cross back to the mainland from Sully Island. Some of them were swept from the causeway by the rip of the tide, which at that point is the one of the highest in the world, second only to Fundy Bay in Nova Scotia.

The first hero of the day was thirteen-year-old John Davies of Connaught Road, Cardiff. He reached safety and although not a strong swimmer went back into the water to help two of his friends who were struggling to beat the tide. John was swept away and drowned and was awarded the Albert Medal posthumously for sacrificing his life.

Margaret Vaughan did not hesitate. She ran over the rocky foreshore into the sea and battled against the fast-flowing tide and currents to bring two Scouts, aged eighteen and eleven, to safety. Rover Scout James Anthony Rees was also involved in the rescue.

A third Scout, eleven-year-old Michael Gleeson of Heathwood Road, Cardiff, was saved by Richard George of Hayes Cottages, Sully. With the help of a non-swimmer he rowed to the rescue.

After the incident Margaret Vaughan told an *Echo* reporter that one of the Scouts she saved jumped on her back while the second clung on to her feet. They were about 30 yards from shore when she reached them and were entangled with their bikes, which they had taken to the island with them. They were all in danger of being swept away, but after a struggle they reached the shore. Margaret was awarded the Albert Medal later that year. The day after the Sully Island incident she was back in the water, representing her school in a gala at Penarth Baths.

With the help of the Victoria Cross and George Medal Association I contacted Margaret at her home in Wiltshire. Now Margaret Purves, at the age of sixty-nine she still swims every morning in her local pool. Modestly she told me that she wasn't sure that she went voluntarily into the sea to rescue the boys or whether she was pushed. She was full of praise for John Davies who lost his life trying to save his friends that day.

Margaret was never a champion swimmer but she did act as a pacemaker for Bristol Channel swimmers, including Jenny James of Pontypridd, who was the first woman to swim the channel both ways.

Two of the Scouts involved in the Sully Island incident were honoured by the Scouts Association. The association's archivist, Patricia Styles, who is based in London, said John Davies's name is on the Scouts' Roll of Honour. He was awarded the Bronze Cross (Posthumous). This is the Scouts' highest award for gallantry and his citation reads: 'Scout John Howard Davies, of the 14th Cardiff (Lord Mayor's Own) Group. In posthumous recognition of his great gallantry in going to the rescue of a boy caught by the tide on the Causeway, Sully, near Cardiff, on May 28, 1949.'

The Bronze Cross was also awarded to another boy who was with the group, Rover Scout James Anthony Rees, also of the 14th Cardiff (Lord Mayor's Own) Group, 'In recognition of his great gallantry in going to the rescue of two boys and assisting others caught by the tide on the Causeway at Sully.'

The stretch of water between Swanbridge and Penarth is one of the most vicious and dangerous in the world at high tide. Many people have died trying to cross from Sully Island. The greatest single disaster along that part of the coast happened on 1 August 1888. A group of soldiers who were camping at Lavernock, the next beach east of Swanbridge, boarded a boat for a trip to Penarth. The boat had too many passengers and seven of the troops, from the 3rd Volunteer Battalion of the Welch Regiment, drowned. There is a memorial to them at Aberfan Cemetery, which was the scene of a solemn military funeral in 1888 – the biggest funeral in the village until 81 of the 144 victims of the Aberfan coal tip disaster were buried there in 1966. The village had suffered two major peacetime disasters seventy-eight years apart.

THE GREAT ESCAPE

No story of Wales and the Second World War would be complete without a report on the Great Escape, not the one depicted in the film of that name but the great escape by German prisoners of war from a camp in South Wales. Journalist Herbert Williams researched the story for his book *Come Out Wherever You Are.** He said:

The Great Escape from Island Farm is a fascinating episode in Welsh history. On the night of 10/11 March 1945, sixty-seven German prisoners of war escaped from Island Farm Camp, Bridgend, through a 60-foot tunnel dug under the wire. It was the biggest escape of German POWs from any British camp in the Second World War. All were recaptured within a week after a massive manhunt involving police, the armed forces and civilians. None got out of Britain but four reached the outskirts of Birmingham and two reached Southampton. Two more were caught near Magor in Monmouthshire. All the rest were recaptured within the old county of Glamorgan, twenty of them being turned in by civilians.

The escapees – mainly officers – were among the thousands of German servicemen captured after D-Day in June 1944. They had made an instant impression by marching smartly to the camp from Bridgend railway station, singing defiantly. They engineered the tunnel cleverly with uprights and cross-sections of timber sawn from the camp's canteen benches. Ventilation was provided by an air line made out of condensed milk tins, with a four-blade fan rotated by a handle.

Digging continued after an earlier tunnel was discovered. Soil was hidden behind a false wall in Hut 9, where the tunnel began. The escapees carried maps

---

* *Come Out Wherever You Are* was first published in 1976 and is to be reissued by Gomer Press. I am grateful to Herbert Williams, a former colleague of mine, for this account, which he has written for this book.

Island Farm, Bridgend.

drawn on shirt tails and handkerchiefs, and compasses made out of magnetised razor blades. The four who reached Birmingham stole a doctor's car parked near the Bridgend camp but abandoned it in the Forest of Dean before hiding in a munitions train. They planned to steal a plane and fly back to Germany.

After the escape, all 1,600 men at Island Farm – designated Camp 198 – were transferred to other POW camps. Their place was taken by high-ranking captives including Field Marshal Gerd von Rundstedt, one of Hitler's senior commanders. The success of the manhunt was a feather in the cap of Superintendent William May of the Glamorgan Constabulary, who devised the master plan for combating a mass escape.

By 2004 only the escape hut – by then a listed building – remained, plus the tunnel itself.

Not a single bomb was dropped on Bridgend during the war; not even an incendiary device, despite the fact that there was an arsenal located in the town. Local people believed this was due to the natural camouflage afforded by the mist that hung over the town like a gigantic curtain. But the 'Great Escape' ensured that Bridgend earned a place in history.

General von Rundstedt, one of the top Nazis imprisoned at Island Farm, at Bridgend.

While the Germans were escaping from Bridgend, Welsh prisoners of war were playing soccer internationals at Stammlager prison camp in Germany. Private Harold Lemon of Tonna, Neath, is standing on the extreme left.

It also has a link with my family. My father, Leading Seaman Denis O'Sullivan, and a shipmate of his from the Cardiff Royal Navy base HMS *Cambria* were each given a rifle and a dozen bullets. Their job was to patrol the beach at Lavernock, between Penarth and Barry, to look out for a German U-boat that might surface to pick up the escaped prisoners. A rifle and a dozen bullets against a U-boat.

IN MEMORY

The names of three local men were not added to the War Memorial in their home area of Crumlin, Monmouthshire, until 4 July 2004. The long-forgotten trio were Stoker First Class John James Webb, Lance Corporal Caleb George Gwilliam and Private Henry Hughes.

Forty-year-old Stoker Webb died when HMS *Orchis* hit a mine off Normandy on 21 August 1944 – five days after depth charges from the corvette sank German U-boat 741 in the same area. *Orchis* was declared a total write-off after limping to Juno Beach, Normandy. The vessel was launched on the Clyde in 1940 and in 1941 became the first British ship to be fitted with Russian radar equipment. Stoker Webb's wife Muriel and his parents Walter and Jane all lived in Crumlin.

Lance Corporal Caleb Gwilliam was only twenty-one when he was killed in Libya on 19 December 1942. He was serving with the Royal Electrical and Mechanical Engineers and was the son of Sidney and Annie, who lived in Treowen, Newbridge. The young NCO is one of 1,214 troops buried in Benghazi Cemetery.

Private Henry Hughes fought with the 3rd Battalion of the Monmouthshire Regiment in Normandy and died 5 miles north of Caen a month and a day after D-Day. The 21-year-old private, the son of Frederick and Beatrice of Newbridge, is buried in St Manvieu War Cemetery, Cheux. Some 49 of the bodies there are still unidentified. Also buried in the cemetery are 536 German troops.

TIME TO CELEBRATE

Eluned 'Freckles' Evans was just eighteen years of age when she joined the Women's Auxiliary Air Force (WAAF) in 1943. She spent her first months as a cook serving up meals to the flying-boat crews at Pembroke Dock and was at RAF St Athan for nearly two years before the end of the war. She was in bed in Hut G2 on the Maintenance Wing when a message came over the tannoy just after midnight on the morning of 8 May 1945. She recalled:

We were told that hostilities in Europe had ceased and the war with Germany was ended. We all cheered, got up and went to the NAAFI where we danced all night. The war may have been over but I had to leave the party at dawn to

The *Western Mail*'s front-page story reporting the end of the war in Europe on 6 May 1945.

report for duty in the cookhouse where I helped to get breakfast for more than 1,000 men.

Eluned and other cooks were still clearing away the lunch dishes when Winston Churchill broadcast to the nation at 3 p.m., confirming that the war was over. It was the longest and happiest day in Eluned's service career, which ended in 1946. She returned to her family home in Abercerdin Road, Evanstown, Gilfach Goch, where she married William Stephens, who had spent the war working down the Britannic Pit, helping to keep the home fires burning.

There were fireworks in Harvey Street, Cadoxton, Barry, and people were singing and dancing in the street following the midnight announcement that Japan had surrendered. My cousin Sid Scales, who then lived in neighbouring Quarella Street, had a rocket left over from the VE celebrations three months earlier. He placed it in a milk bottle, put a match to it and it shot right across the road, through the window of a house and set a bed on fire. Fortunately no one was hurt as the rocket went through the middle window, right between the elderly couple who were sitting on the bed. The couple, whose name was Munn,

A VE Day party in Gray Street, Aberaman.

Reason to celebrate: a street party in Stafford Street, Grangetown.

Celebrating in Butetown, Cardiff. *(Cardiff City Library)*

All smiles in Butetown at the end of the war. *(Cardiff City Library)*

had come to Barry after their home in Dover had been shelled by the Germans, who had targeted the White Cliffs area with their big guns in the early days of the war.

The incident failed to spoil the party, which went on until the early hours of the morning. Many of the youngsters belonged to Madam Collins Rosita Accordion Band and they provided the music for the older folk to dance and sing. Harvey Street, where I was born in number 30 on 29 December 1934, was like a village and most people in the area were related by blood or marriage. They were always looking for a reason for a knees-up, whether it was a royal occasion or a wartime victory.

The VE and VJ celebrations were extra-special and are rich in the memories of all those who were there. After the VJ party we got back to bed around dawn, only to be awoken 10 minutes later by two happy young men who knocked on every door to tell us the war was over!

Epilogue

by PETER BIBBY

Peter Bibby, Community Affairs Editor of the South Wales Echo, *joined Welsh veterans on a pilgrimage in June 2004. The nostalgic journey was made to mark the sixtieth anniversary of D-Day, 6 June 1944, when 150,000 Allied troops landed in Normandy at the start of an eleven-month battle to defeat Hitler's Germany. Readers contributed to the expenses of the former servicemen as part of Operation Echo. The anniversary ceremonies were watched by millions on television. This is part of Peter's moving account of the occasion.*

It took 60 long years for retired carpenter Arthur Jones to say goodbye to his brother who died a D-Day hero. It was during Operation Echo that he finally found the Normandy grave that for years had carried the name of an Unknown Soldier. Former RAF Servicing Commando Arthur, now 80, joined Operation Echo determined to track down the final resting place of his brother Bill. And he did – in Bayeux Cemetery, among the 3,843 who lost their lives in the first few weeks of the D-Day landings. Bill was just 19 when his South Wales Borderers, the only Welsh unit to land on D-Day itself, came under fierce fire near the Normandy village of Asnelles. They were just 24 hours into the Normandy campaign when Bill was shot and left by the roadside as his comrades fled the pursuing Germans.

Exactly where and when he died will never be known, but back home in Norfolk Street, Canton, Cardiff, his worried parents Samuel and Olive Jones were told their son was missing in action. It was to be months before they discovered his fate. It was to be another 11 years, in 1955, that the remains in grave B4 in section 24 of one of the biggest war cemeteries in Europe, were identified as those of the Cardiff teenager. Until then his body had been lying in a grave marked as *Known Only to God*. Arthur, of Lime Grove, Pentrebane, Cardiff, as he laid his hand on his brother's headstone said: 'It's hard to believe that after all these years I am here again with him. I've never been one for visiting cemeteries, but I'm so pleased to have found him at last. Bill was such a great kid. We weren't just brothers, we were friends and we'd go walking for miles together. He was too young to die, such a waste of a life.'

Arthur, who went to Normandy himself five weeks after Bill's death, had a special inscription written for the headstone that marks his brother's grave. It reads: *Private William George Jones. The South Wales Borderers 7th June 1944. Age 19. In cherished memory of dear Bill. He died so very young. Always remembered.*

The 60th anniversary was a day that meant so much to the generation that had given so much. Thousands of D-Day veterans took part in two major events to mark . . . the Normandy landings that heralded the start of the liberation of Europe after five years of war. And no one was left in any doubt after a sun-soaked service at the Bayeux War Graves Cemetery and an emotional afternoon re-enactment and parade in Arromanches – the Band of Brothers were back. If the Bayeux Cemetery with its line upon line of headstones was a stark reminder of the real fruits of war, Arromanches 2004 was the proud veterans' day in the sun. . . .

Some looked reluctant heroes, while others basked in the well-deserved limelight. Here were ordinary husbands, fathers, grandfathers, great-grandfathers and widowers being treated like stars. And the years rolled away as they marched proudly through the town to meet the Queen. All weekend, wherever they went in France this special D-Day Band of Brothers were given a hero's welcome. Sad then, that when they get home to resume their lives as ordinary pensioners, they return to a life of second-class citizens.

Seventy-eight-year-old Tony Pengelly of Wern Goch Road, Cyncoed, took part in one of the most poignant parts of the anniversary events. Just a couple of hundred veterans from all over the UK were picked for the march of remembrance through the Normandy seaside town of Arromanches. And Tony was one of those selected. He landed on D-Day and within weeks found his ability to speak French came in handy. He was detailed as interpreter to *Daily Herald* war photographer Jack Easten. After leaving the Army Tony worked as a civil servant at the Welsh Office.

Barbara Thomas, of Portskewett, who joined the *Echo* party with her husband Ainsley, learnt for the first time on the journey what had happened to her 19-year-old brother Laurence, who died in the Normandy fighting. The man sitting in front of her on the coach had been in the same regiment as Barbara's brother and was in the same battle in which Laurence was killed. He was able to give details the family had wondered about for 60 years.

Brothers Roy and Cliff O'Neill were in the same unit in the South Wales Borderers, landed on D-Day and went from Normandy through Belgium, Holland and into Germany. They made a pact never to be in the same trench together. 'That way we thought at least one of us might survive – and we were both lucky enough to both come home in one piece,' said 80-year-old Roy, of Croft-y-Genau Road, St Fagans.

Irene Robson, of Caerleon Road, Dinas Powys, told how her late husband John was in Caen on D-Day. He was with the 6th Airborne Royal Divisional

Signals and, having completed 200 jumps, he trained several hundred other parachutists. The couple married in March 1946. John wrote about his 12 years in the Royal Corps of Signals and his books are now in the Imperial War Museum, London.

Eric Powell, of Penygraig, Rhondda, told how he came home from school on the day before D-Day to find there was no sign of the American sergeant who had been billeted at his home. He also noticed that the church hall, which was being used as a mess hall and cook house, was all locked up. His family heard afterwards that the Americans had all gone to Barry to board the D-Day ships. His mother went to Sergeant Meirion's bedroom and on the dressing table found a letter with some of his personal things. The family heard later that he had been killed during the first wave of the assault on the Normandy beaches, one of thousands of Allied troops who died in that historic battle and on the killing fields between Normandy and Nazi Germany.

Acknowledgements

This book would not have been possible without the help and support given by many people including:

Barry Town Council; Nick Beatie; John Beynon, Honorary Curator, Tenby Museum; Peter Bibby, Community Affairs Editor, *South Wales Echo*; the staff at Caerphilly (especially Susan Lewis), Ebbw Vale, Newport, Shrewsbury and Swansea libraries; Commonwealth War Graves Commission; John Iorwerth Davies; Downside School archive; Martin Everett, Curator South Wales and Monmouthshire Regimental Museum Brecon; Simon Farrington, Editor in Chief, *Celtic Press* and Chief Librarian, *Western Mail and Echo*; Paul Flynn MP; Allan George; Glamorgan County Cricket Club archive; Steve Groves, BBC; Andrew Hignell, author of *Turnbull, a Welsh Sporting Hero*; Imperial War Museum; Bryn Jones, former head of local studies at Cardiff Central Library, and the staff there; The Kingsland Singers (Mary Taylor, Enid Craven, Maureen Nelson and Captain Ray Brinkworth); Brian Lee, racing expert and author; Brian Luxton; Alastair Milburn, Editor, *South Wales Echo* (who gave me permission to quote from *Bombers Over Wales*; Roger Morrisy, Editor, *Celtic Press*; Bernard Murray, President of the Whitchurch branch of the Royal British Legion; National Archives; Frank Prendergast, former BBC engineer; RAF Museum, Hendon; Royal National Lifeboat Institution; James Stewart, HTV; Pat Styles, Archivist, Boy Scouts Association; Barry Tobin; Victoria Cross and George Cross Association; John and Phyllis Wells; *Western Mail and Echo* library staff – Tony Woolway, Robert Mager, Edwina Turner and Maria Jorge; Herbert Williams, author of *Come Out Wherever You Are*; Stuart Williams; Colin Yaxley, National Maritime Museum

There are still many stories of the war to be told and readers are invited to send their personal memories or stories of their relatives or friends to John O'Sullivan, c/o Sutton Publishing, Phoenix Mill, Thrupp, Stroud, Gloucestershire, GL5 2BU.